Dreams

from the Other Side

Dreams
from the Other Side

Messages of Love from Beyond the Veil

Alex Lukeman, Ph.D.

M. Evans and Company, Inc.
New York

M. Evans and Company, Inc.
216 East 49th Street
New York, New York 10017

Library of Congress Cataloging-in-Publication Data

Lukeman, Alex, 1941–
        Dreams from the other side : messages of love from beyond the veil /
    Alex Lukeman.
            p.   cm.
        Includes bibliographical references and index.
        ISBN 0-87131-969-1
        1. Dreams. 2. Dream interpretation. 3. Spiritual life. I. Title.
        BF1091 .L825 2002
        154.6'32—dc21   2002016108

Printed in the United States of America

9   8   7   6   5   4   3   2   1

Contents

◆••◆••◆••◆••◆••◆••◆••◆••◆••◆••◆••◆••◆••◆••◆••◆••◆••◆••◆•

This book would not be possible without the contributions of hundreds of dreamers. I have changed their names to protect their anonymity. I want to thank all of them for sharing these powerful stories of love with me.

◆••◆••◆••◆••◆••◆••◆••◆••◆••◆••◆••◆••◆••◆••◆••◆••◆••◆••◆•

Never the Spirit is born
The Spirit will cease to be never
Never was time it was not
End and beginning are dreams
Birthless and deathless and changeless
Remains the Spirit forever
Death has not touched it at all
Dead though the house of it seems
                    —*Bhagavad Gita*
                    (translation by Sir Edwin Arnold)

Introduction

•◆•

I USED TO BE A SKEPTIC about the idea that loved ones who have passed through the veil could visit us in our dreams. I was sure dreams in which someone appeared to return were attempts by a grieving psyche to compensate for the loss of a loved one, a way for the heart to heal what the mind could not accept. Many dreams and stories over the years have made me change my mind. I am no longer a skeptic.

Part of my journey to belief required giving up rigid perceptions I had formed about what was real and what was not. God knows, there have been enough events and phenomena in my life to convince anyone that things are not what they appear to be. However I am a stubborn individual, and, like most of us, I fight to hold on to my ideas even when faced with strong evidence I am wrong. It's human nature. Before I could accept that the dead return in dreams, I had to come to terms with my own issues about death and challenge my ideas about what lies beyond death's gate.

Beliefs about God, spirit, and life after death form at an early age. Mine were of a conventional, Christian type, imprinted on my mind during regular Sunday school and church attendance. One of those beliefs was that the dead do not return. To my young mind it seemed that there was an inherent conflict between the idea of resurrection and eternal life and assertions that the dead cannot return to the living. But who was I to argue?

Such beliefs are crucial cornerstones propping up our view of reality. It usually takes something undeniable and out of the ordinary to change them. For me, it took a near-death experience, followed by several years of confrontation with extra-ordinary phenomena and realities I could not ignore.

There is a strange and wonderful truth: When someone we love passes through death's door to the other side, he or she can return to us in spirit, in our dreams. We may not have scientific proof, but there are many stories of return, shared over thousands of years by people like you and me.

What happens after we die? The only thing we know for sure is that death comes to us all, and that when it does, something changes. We may not know what lies on the other side, but people all over the world believe in existence beyond death. Many believe someone has contacted them from the other side. Some visitations take the form of ghostly sightings, others as mysterious phone calls, electrical phenomena, or strangely moving objects. By far the largest number of contacts happens in dreams.

Anyone who has felt the grief of a loved one's passing knows it takes considerable time for healing. When the beloved returns in a dream, it has a profound effect on our emotional well-being. We wake knowing the person we love is still present, still available to us. The dreams reassure us that we, too, will survive the inevitability of death.

Introduction

It is clear to me that those on the other side are able to visit us in our dreams. When they do, advice is given, forgiveness becomes reality, and love brings completion and acceptance to the dreamer. In every culture, people see such dreams as a genuine doorway to the other side. Not only visitations take place. Some people have dreams foreshadowing physical death; others have dreams of spiritual beings bringing messages of comfort and wisdom.

Much of my work over the last twenty-some years has focused on dreams. Dreams provide a rich and truthful resource for understanding who we are. Many times people told me dreams of loved ones gone who came to them in the night. Over time, I came to see many of these dreams as more than just the workings of a mind trying to heal itself of emotional pain and loss.

It is true some dreams of the departed are psychological in nature, a way for us to deal with emotions like grief or anger. With these dreams, it is not necessary to look for a mysterious or otherworldly explanation. They have a different feel to them; the kinds of events that occur are different from what I would call true dreams of return. In true dreams of return, a sense of completion and deep connection is always present. A psychological dream may present images of the departed, but there is no resolution for the living.

In thousands of years of human history, each culture and time has come up with its own version of what happens when we die, and each has ideas about what it means when the dead return. I could not possibly include all of those ideas here, but I have tried to give a sense of how different cultures and societies think about these kinds of dreams. The differing beliefs form a background tapestry for the stories you will read here.

Dreams from the Other Side is about dreams and messages from the dimension beyond death. They come from the spiritual realm, in every sense of the word. Here you will find dreams and visions that comfort us and help us realize that death is not what it appears to be. They are gifts to our troubled minds, holding out the promise of life after death and helping to prepare us for our own transition when the time comes.

So many people have dreams like this. So many of us believe we have contacted loved ones gone on before. In the United States alone, over 50 million people feel they have touched the other side. Not all of them are delusional, under the effect of medications, or sensation seekers; nor do they fit any other rationale offered to explain their experience of the beyond. If you are one of these people, you are not alone.

Contact with the other side can change us forever. Something in us breathes a sigh of relief when we have such a dream. Fear retreats, the natural fear of our own death and of the unknown experience waiting beyond death's gateway. We find comfort and peace, perhaps a healing respite from the grief of a loved one's passing.

The stories in this book are all true, changing or affecting people's lives in real ways. Many are dreams of loved ones who returned to the dreamer days, months, or even years after death. All are dreams that reassured and inspired the dreamers.

Dreams that tell us all is well with our departed loved ones bring resolution and closure in a way that nothing else can quite achieve. Things are said in dreams left unspoken in real life, bringing a sense of completion missing until that moment. Unlike most dreams, which vanish upon waking, these are remembered.

If you have dreams like this, perhaps you will find confirmation in these pages for what you already know or suspect to be true. The souls of those who have gone before return in our dreams, bringing messages of love and hope from the other side.

The dreams in these pages come from all sorts of different people with something unusual in common. Their dreams connected them to spirit and gave them certain knowledge that they were not alone. They are not, and neither are you.

Someday we will all know exactly what stands on the other

Introduction

side. Until then, we have only dreams and memories, tales brought to us from a far and distant place by travelers who return briefly with the dust of the other side clinging to their clothes and shoes.

Alex Lukeman
Fort Collins, Colorado

Dreams

from the Other Side

Chapter 1

The Other Side

Our Creator would never have made such lovely days,
And have given us the deep hearts to enjoy them,
Unless we were meant to be immortal.

— NATHANIEL HAWTHORNE

D O THE DEAD RETURN to us in dreams? Do our loved ones who have passed on come back to us with messages of love and comfort? In short and simple terms, the answer is yes. Let me tell you a dream that shows what I mean.

As her mother lay dying, Amelia's father was unable to face the chore of packing up his wife's possessions. He sent his daughter to handle the job, to the house he had built for retirement just two years before. As she drove north to the house, Amelia felt her mother's passing. A phone call confirmed her mother had died. At the house that night, she had a vivid dream.

In the dream, her mother appeared and guided Amelia through the house. Here are Amelia's words.

The Door in the Attic

I dreamt of my mother. She led me by the hand from room to room and showed me where to find her "special" belongings. With great love, mother told me how to dispose of each item; who should receive what inheritance, of pearls, rings, or a shawl from her honeymoon. Then, in the dream, she led me to the attic and pointed to an almost imperceptible door in the back of a crawl space. The dream ended.

The next day, after sorting and packing through things according to her mother's wishes in the dream, Amelia decided to explore the attic. Crawling through the boxes and cobwebs, she saw the small door of her dream barely visible in the gloom. She opened the door and found a box. In the box was a packet of old love letters written between her mother and father. For Amelia, this was a heartfelt gift of love.

Amelia had never been in the attic and was not familiar with the house. She had no knowledge of the small door and the crawlspace behind it, or of the box of letters. If her mother did not come to her in that dream, how else can you explain this true story? Sometimes the living learn something they could not know in any other way from the loved one who appears in the dream. Such dreams are dramatic proof the dead return to us in dreams.

It took a near-death experience in 1975 to make me understand that death is not the final event it appears to be. One hot July evening, I walked slowly into the emergency ward of a busy New York hospital, struggling for breath, with severe pain in my chest radiating down my left arm—classic signs of a heart attack. I was thirty-four years old. Within minutes of entering the hospital, I was flat on my back, wired to machines, breathing oxygen. People were running around looking serious and worried. I knew I was in big trouble.

I had contracted pericarditis, a viral infection of the lining around the heart. The pericardial sac was filling with fluid, compressing my heart and squeezing the life from me. There are no drugs for that. The only treatment given to me was Tylenol. My life was out of control and under the supervision of others. There was nothing I could do except surrender to what was meant to happen.

Hours later, I was in a deep and dreamless sleep when I suddenly came fully awake. My mind was clear, aware, and alert, but my body was a different story. I felt exhausted, used up, depleted. It was an enormous effort just to move my eyes. What had woken me?

From my raised hospital bed I could see several glass cubicles, identical to mine, arranged in a semicircle around a central station. Everyone I could see in those cubicles looked very, very ill. Dials and moving readouts glowed in the dim light. Intricate spider webs of wires, tubes, and IV drips dangled over every still figure. It was a scene straight from a medical horror movie. Only it was not a movie—it was reality. I was in one of the inner sanctums of the medical profession, the ICU, a place created to provide a last bastion against death.

The big clock over the central nurses' station said 3:00 A.M. I looked at the clock and saw that the second hand was not moving. That's very strange, I thought. Then I became aware that something was in the room with me. In the corner of the room, I saw a shimmering, vibrating column of beautiful rose-red light, reaching from the floor to the ceiling. About three feet wide, the column of light was translucent—I could see shapes through it but not details. An electric sense of energy and presence filled the room. It vibrated. It was alive, sentient.

I knew without doubt, I was looking at death in that strange light.

I felt perfectly calm. Unbidden, my mind began a life review as I lay there gazing on the column of rosy light. Thoughts and scenes, memories and sounds, people and situations long forgotten cascaded in vivid color across the screen of my mind's eye, folding in on one another in rapid sequence.

1975 was the year I hit the wall. I had reached a point in life without joy or meaning. My relationships, my work—everything—felt meaningless and destructive to me. There was nothing pulling me forward into life, nothing worthwhile to live for. Lying there in the presence of that rosy death-light, I knew with certainty that I had a choice. I could continue to live or I could let go into the mystery of the light and die. Either way was all right; either way was correct. I knew that letting go into the light was not an end, but rather a transition into some other kind of existence. I cannot explain how I knew this, but there was no question it was so. Meanwhile, the scenes of my life continued to pour through my awareness.

Time and space felt suspended in a place of clear, calm detachment, as I gazed on that shimmering column of light. I could feel something within me deciding whether to go or to stay, but it was not a rational process. Somewhere along the way, I felt a decision to stay and complete, without any idea of what I was supposed to be completing. At just that exact instant, the column of rosy light grew bigger, expanding outward through the room, and disappeared. As it vanished, the monitor sounded an alarm and the night nurse rushed into the cubicle. She looked so worried, but I knew I would be all right. The central clock still said 3:00 A.M., but the second hand was moving again and time was no longer suspended.

My life took a different track that morning. Since that day, I do not feel the same way about death. I don't want to think about the inevitability of friends and loved ones passing, I don't like the idea of pain and discomfort in my final hours, but I no longer fear. I know, because of my experience, that death is not an end but a doorway into some other dimension of existence.

With the appearance of the light in my hospital cubicle, my

life changed dramatically. I ended my destructive relationships and began a long period of self-discovery. I began a learning journey in psychology and alternative healing. I discovered a commitment to spiritual self-exploration and expression. I discovered I could understand dreams, and people have been telling them to me ever since.

Many of the people who share dreams in these pages did not believe in life after death before they had the dream. Many of them had lost faith—faith in themselves, faith in God (by whatever name), and faith in the idea of meaning or purpose for life. I was one of those people, until that column of rosy light convinced me of the reality of life after death in ways that words never could. I got a direct look at the other side.

THE OTHER SIDE

The phrase "other side" is attributed to Emanuel Swedenborg.* A Swedish philosopher, scientist, theologian, and mystic, he was one of the great lights of the eighteenth century. In using this term, Swedenborg was referring to all things that exist beyond our usual limits of awareness, on the other side of death's passage. Visits from the dead, the appearance of angels, divine visitations, and clear instructions from spirit are all from the other side. All of these may come to us in dreams.

Dreams are not the only gateway to the other side. It is possible for us to encounter the other side while awake and alert as well. Beginning with that day in the hospital, I have experienced many extraordinary phenomena. All have reinforced my belief in other dimensions and realities that defy rational explanation. None of these other realities can be subjected to the rigors of scientific proof, but all can be experienced as real, even verified by

---

*Emanuel Swedenborg (1688–1772) was at the forefront of scientific and literary thinking during his time. He spent the last part of his life focused on theology and the mystical connection with the divine.

others who may be witnesses when the door to the other side opens.

I have been fortunate, meeting some unusual people with a variety of healing and intuitive gifts. I saw a silver-haired woman in Hawaii walk dry through the falling rain, while everyone beside her was soaked. The rain simply did not fall on her, only on us. A true shaman in the Hawaiian tradition, a genuine kahuna, she was famous for her ability to stand at the shore and call the creatures of the sea to her feet.

Once I watched a young woman dying with terminal cancer, dreaming unknowingly in a radiant sphere of unearthly, beautiful light. A magnificent healing vortex of swirling energy and numinous images surrounded the table on which she lay. Streams of light and energy poured through my hands and into her body. A healer who had opened the door to this context of spirit and divine energy stood benignly at the head of the table, holding the focus for the rest of us. She recovered.

I have seen people diagnosed with days or weeks to live recover fully from terminal illness. I have seen burns and tumors disappear as I watched. I saw a holy man in India sweep a crowd of thousands with a tangible, powerful energy of love from his eyes, then materialize from thin air exactly what was needed for the person sitting at his feet. I've heard stories and dreams of emotional, spiritual, and physical healing. Some of the most powerful dreams came from people visited by dear ones who had passed through death's divide, bearing messages of love and comfort.

These things have taught me that life is not exactly what it appears to be. We are living in a world filled with mystery, a world imbued with spirit and love. It is a world where unseen dimensions exist and overlap each other. The passport into those dimensions is our consciousness—the very thing that imbues us with a sense of self and life.

CONSCIOUSNESS & DREAMS

"Consciousness" is a word much abused in the literature of the human potential movement, but that does not mean it is a word we can ignore. Precisely because it is impossible to define consciousness to everyone's satisfaction, the search for something that enhances our experience of being conscious, whatever that may mean, has become big business. Gurus of consciousness abound, some wonderful, some not.

The path to increased awareness is a path of spiritual discovery. There isn't any particular way to spirit, which exists everywhere. Spirit is independent of theology and structure. We can stand and sing in a Four Square Gospel church, sit quietly and watch the sun rise, or bathe in the Ganges, and spirit will be there.

Spirit provides endless opportunities for discovery, countless surprises that challenge us to open our minds and hearts. Often it takes some powerful experience, like my encounter with a rose-colored angel of death and light, to get us to pay attention. It can also take the form of a dream or a dream message that we cannot deny. Dreams are a way consciousness beyond our normal limits can make itself known.

Dreams are one of the common threads that tie us all together. Everyone dreams. If something prevents us from dreaming, bad things happen to our sanity. We begin hallucinating and acting in bizarre ways. We don't have to remember our dreams, as far as our physical and mental health are concerned, but we have to have them. We all dream, whether or not we remember our dreams.

Whether or not dreams have any meaning is a subject of controversy today, but it has not always been that way. For thousands of years, people in many different cultures thought of dreams as messages from the divine gods or from the spirits of the dead. The classical Greek word for dreams meant "message."

25

With the emergence of Christianity as the major religion of the West, dreams fell into disrepute. There was great fear among early theologians that dreams might be a gateway for the devil's work. These fears arose partially from mistaken translations of phrases and words in the Bible, generally attributed to St. Jerome.* New and more accurate translations of the Bible correcting those old mistakes are now becoming widely available. It is ironic to condemn dreams, in light of the many wonderful revelations and dream teachings found in the Old Testament and elsewhere in Christian literature.

The ancient Egyptians, the Greeks of the classic period, the Romans, the ancient Chinese, and the world of Islam all believed in the power and truth of dreams. To them, dreams were especially important when they contained messages from angels or the spirits of the dead.

Angels and visions appearing in dreams have inspired world religion. Buddha's mother dreamed a white elephant embraced her, penetrating her side with his trunk, signaling conception of a holy being. The prophet Muhammad received the teachings of Islam, including the text of the Koran, in dreams. In a dream the angel Gabriel sent Muhammad out of exile and inspired him to lead an army against Mecca. An angel revealed the Book of Mormon to Joseph Smith, the patriarch of Mormonism. Christ visited the emperor Constantine in a dream, giving him a sign that led to victory in battle and the establishment of Christianity as the official religion of the Roman Empire.

You don't have to believe in these religious teachings to see that dreams can shape the destiny of millions. The suppression of dreams in the West as the work of the devil was part of the superstitious and unenlightened thinking of the Dark and

---

*Author of the official Latin version (Vulgate) of the Bible, Jerome incorrectly translated the Hebrew text in Deuteronomy and Leviticus to condemn "observing dreams." His mistranslation may have been deliberate. The result was that trying to understand dreams became the equivalent of practicing witchcraft. Please see footnote regarding Robert Van de Castle's book on dreams.

Middle Ages. The legacy continues today. Many still dismiss ' dreams as nonsense, despite thousands of years of anecdotal evidence to the contrary.

Some argue that dreams have little or no relevance for our daily lives. Dreams of loved ones returning from the other side and comforting those left behind are even more provocative to someone who gives dreams no credibility. It doesn't really matter what skeptics think about it. What matters is the emotional healing and personal peace that accompany such dreams.

The discussion about what happens after death will never be settled, at least while we are still alive! Every spiritual and religious philosophy has something to say about it, and most do not agree. Most of us want to believe in some form of ongoing existence, and most people in the world believe there is spiritual purpose for our lives that becomes clear when we die.

Many people and cultures honor dreams of the dead as genuine visits from beyond death's divide. Some, like the Aboriginal people of Australia, believe there is no separation between life and death. This life and the next are seen as one continuous state of being, inextricably entwined together. A dream of someone who has "died" is just a visit, as if the person came in and sat down for a nice conversation. Most of us, though, see death as a final, irrevocable, personal reality. That has given rise to many ideas and beliefs about the existence of something that survives death—the soul.

Excavations of burial sites from prehistoric times reveal that the earliest peoples believed in some form of continuing life after death. Flowers, food, comforting objects for the journey into the unknown, weapons, clothing, and religious objects are frequently unearthed in ancient graves, even as far back as Neanderthal man. We are not so different from those ancient people; the mystery of what happens to us at death still fascinates humankind.

Dreams are a common thread woven into the tapestry of spiritual teaching about life after death from all times and places. The dream may be welcome or not, but the historical consensus is that the dead can return in dreams. Contemporary scientific thought on the subject is predictable and rigid, ranging from extreme skepticism to absolute denial of such a possibility. Who can blame the scientist? The nature of science demands proof, which, in this case, can never be determined. All that can be recorded is the anecdotal stories of those who have had such dreams, coupled with their subjective responses, which are deeply conditioned by cultural and religious background. Dreams and stories do not lend themselves well to scientific inquiry. The good news for those who have healing dreams of departed loved ones is that proof is not required.

There are many historical anecdotes of the dead returning in dreams to provide guidance and advice. Some may be simply good stories, handed down over the centuries and embellished along the way. Some anecdotes seem well documented and have an eerie ring of truth. One of my favorites involves Dante, the master poet of the fourteenth century, who composed *Inferno* and *Paradiso*.[1]

Paradiso appeared incomplete on Dante's death. The manuscript lacked the final thirteen cantos, and attempts to find the missing pages were unsuccessful. Eight months after his father's death, Dante's son Jacobo had a powerful dream. In the dream, his father appeared. Father and son had a pleasant discussion about the nature of the afterlife. Then Dante touched a spot on the wall of a room where he had slept when alive. Dante told Jacobo that what he was looking for would be found there.

Even in a time when dreams were publicly condemned, no one would ignore a dream like that. Jacobo went to his father's house and found the missing thirteen cantos concealed in a niche in the wall.

Unlike historical stories that may or may not be true, the dreams and stories in this book are certainly true, anecdotes told by average people leading everyday lives. Eventually all of us must deal with the reality of death and the absence of someone we care for or love. These tales hold out a promise: Death is not the end, but a gateway into another dimension of existence. Those we love can and do return to us, helping us come to terms with our feelings of loss and sadness.

Perhaps the easiest way to cross the divide between life and death is through our dreams. As we sleep, the veil between the worlds grows thin. When the barriers are down, souls may slip easily between the different realities. Dreams provide a bridge between here and the other side, a vehicle the departed can use to contact us.

THE SOUL

You are not going to get the ultimate description of soul out of me! The best of human philosophers, literary geniuses, and theologians have been arguing about it for thousands of years. There are a lot of people who talk about the soul as if they know exactly what it is all about, but I am not one of them. All I know is that it is a mystery, perhaps a mystery even greater than what happens when we die. After my 3:00 A.M. visit with death, I am also certain of one other thing: Something in us goes on after life ends. It is the essence of our spiritual being. The essence can return in dreams, after death has taken the physical form.

You cannot find a good definition of the soul by looking in Webster's dictionary. The best they can come up with is ". . . a spirit, embodied or disembodied: innermost being or nature."[2] Ideas about what the soul is and what happens to it at death depend on the time and culture of the person trying to understand the soul's nature. In our world of cell phones and sixty-hour workweeks, there is little emphasis on making sense of the nature of the soul. Soul study is not high on most people's list of priorities.

The ancient Chinese and the Greeks of the classical age thought the soul left the body at night during sleep, wandering far, enjoying many experiences and activities. This belief exists today in metaphysical teachings about astral travel or soul journeying through dreams. Many traditions and countless spiritual teachings say the soul can lift out of the physical body, either during sleep or when practicing some form of spiritual discipline or meditation. If the soul can leave the body, it must have independent existence. If soul consciousness is independent of the body, the soul of someone who has died may continue to exist after death. That would follow, since the soul is not dependent on physical form. Death may end our physical existence, but it does not end our consciousness.

In the end, none of the arguments about the existence and nature of the soul matter much. What matters is the reality of the soul's survival after death. Each of us comes to acceptance of the soul's existence in our own way. We discover it through spiritual practice, a near-death experience, or even a dream.

The earliest descriptions of the soul come to us from ancient Egypt. The Egyptians wrote down their beliefs in the Book of the Dead, describing an elaborate afterlife and underworld journey for the soul. It is the first written work detailing a culture's spiritual beliefs about the afterlife. The text contains careful instructions to prepare the reader for safe passage. Egyptians believed the gods measured and weighed the deeds of the living after death, and that lightness of heart was the most important factor in determining the fate of the soul. We might say that the most important factors are love and compassion.

Another famous text on the afterlife is the Tibetan Book of the Dead. This book likewise gives detailed descriptions and spiritual instructions for the soul's journey after death. In our own culture, we have no formal book of the dead, although there are many grim theological descriptions of purgatory, heaven, and hell. We do have many religious instructions for the living, designed to guide us safely to the other side.

Every culture has a teaching about life after death, and each offers a picture of what to expect when the soul leaves the body. Each also has some idea about what happens to people who are good and who are not so good, as defined by the values of the culture.

Records exist from the earliest times of people who have died returning in dreams, of near-death experiences and visions of the dead. They all have one thing in common: a message that something in us survives after death. If needed, sometimes we can return from the other side to comfort and help the living. How it happens, or what determines the need, remains a mystery.

THE QUESTION OF PSYCHOLOGICAL COMPENSATION

Psychological compensation is what occurs when we do something to balance feelings of loss or inadequacy. Compensation can be conscious or unconscious. In the case of dreams, we are talking about an unconscious process. When we compensate, we are attempting to shift the inner emotional or psychological balance to an opposite pole. Oddly, this can occur even when things are going well. For example, a man in a position of exalted power and responsibility might have a dream of being helpless and small. Compensation is a kind of psychic inner scale that can weigh the perceptions and realities of our egos and our lives and adjust the balance as needed. One of the best places to see compensation in action is in dreams.

Dreams of the departed can be seen as a form of compensation. The dreamer has an experience of reunion and feels better. From a psychological point of view, that's all there is to it—just an attempt by a wounded psyche to try to resolve a painful, unacceptable situation.

If you prefer, you can consider a dream of saying goodbye to an old friend as a psychological dream of compensation. Does it matter to the dreamer? I think not. What counts is the feeling of resolution and completion that comes with the dream. Whether or not the old friend returned, the result is the same. However, psychological compensation does not explain how someone can return in a dream and point out the hiding place of a box of love letters or the missing chapters of a manuscript. It doesn't explain dreams like the ones at the beginning of the next chapter, where the dying appear to friends and family before anyone knows they are dead.

DREAM SYMBOLS

Sometimes we have dreams where the dead appear because they make a good symbol for something we need to think about. They are not returning, but our dreaming mind uses the image of the dead person to get something across to our waking awareness. All regular dreams are composed of symbols, and everything in our life experience can provide imagery for them. That includes people who have passed on.

It is perfectly possible to have a dream about a deceased parent, friend, or other without it meaning that the dead person has come back. If I dream about my father, who died many years ago, it is just as likely that my dreaming mind is trying to tell me something about feelings and perceptions inside myself. My father can represent many things and is a complicated dream symbol.

Think about this for a moment. Any person who shows up in a dream represents much more than just the appearance of a character on our inner stage. People are not simple (well, most people anyway), and as dream symbols, they can represent all of the qualities, ideas about life, and ways of relating to us that they exhibit, or exhibited, in real life. That means that if I dream about my father, I am reminded of all the things that make up my experience of him as a human being and as a parent—good, bad, and indifferent.

Going a little further with this, I have to think through which of his many qualities expressed themselves in the dream. Is he friendly, supportive, judgmental, authoritative, helpless, arrogant, or something else? My father could be all of those things. Once I identify the qualities, I can take the next step and add them into the mix of feelings and ideas that can lead to interpreting the dream.

It is not my purpose here to try to show you how to interpret dreams. I only bring up the example of parents and others who appear in dreams because of the need to talk about the difference between regular dreams and true dreams of return. If you are interested in interpreting dreams, please see one of my other books, *What Your Dreams Can Teach You* (M. Evans, 2001), and you will learn more about it.

TRUE DREAMS OF RETURN

How do you tell the difference between a psychological dream and a true dream of return? The answer is highly subjective and varies from one person to another, but you can look for common markers reported by many dreamers.

True dreams of return have several powerful characteristics that set them apart from ordinary dreams. Not all of these markers will be present in every dream. It is possible for some of them, like a heightened sense of color and feeling, to appear in dreams that have nothing to do with someone returning from the other side. Just the same, if you dream of a loved one coming back to you in a dream and the dream contains some of these elements, then the chances are good it is the real thing.

Common Markers of True Dreams of Return

• You receive information you could not know in other ways, and can confirm the information at a future date.

• You receive support and resolution for something bothering you, especially if it involves personal relationships or an important decision. This can happen when you wish your loved one was present to advise you, or you wish you could share some personal success or joy with your loved one.

• You receive a warning about something. It could be an event, illness, or situation representing potential upheaval or upset in your life. In these kinds of dreams, someone lets you know about potential or real trouble on the way. You might get a chance to ask questions, and you can trust the answers.

• The feeling of the dream is significantly different from your regular, everyday dreams. True dreams of return have a distinct and tangible feeling of connection and reality. You can characterize them by feelings of relief, joy, comfort, and love. Especially love. That different feeling, hard to describe, is a major marker of dreams coming from beyond the veil.

• You know in the dream that it is not just a dream.

• The setting may be undefined, misty, and cloudy.

- There is an indescribable feeling of "knowing" that the person "has to go."

- You awaken feeling happy and calm, joyful at seeing your loved one again.

- The person who returns has a wonderful look of youthfulness, vibrancy, and well-being.

- There is a change in your regular dream perspective, especially regarding color. If you usually dream in black and white, the dream will be in color. If you always dream in color, the colors become heightened, enhanced, vivid, and electric.

- The dream produces change in your outer, waking life. It could be a change of mind about something or a "change of heart." A true dream of return affects us in a way no ordinary dream can ever do.

- You awaken realizing that some old pattern of thought or perception is no longer valid. For example, you realize you no longer have to get the approval of a parent or other important figure that appeared in the dream.

- The behavior of the person who appears in the dream is consistent with their real-life personality. A psychological dream is more likely to present the image as a character in your own play, with less emphasis on the typical behavior the person actually showed in real life.

Love is the key when considering dreams from the other side. We are loved and we have always been loved, but we forget this spiritual truth. It is easy to forget, because we get caught up in the struggles and daily challenges of life. Meeting deadlines, paying the rent, getting the car to the shop, dealing with annoying situations—all of these mundane things and more take over our attention and our focus. We forget we are more than just people going about our business and doing our best to get by. When someone returns in our dreams and reminds us that life goes on after death, we get a chance to reconnect to more than the person who is gone. We feel the breath of eternity and a spiritual promise we cannot deny.

GRIEF

Grief is devastating. None of us knows exactly how we will deal with grief if it comes. There are as many ways to deal with grief as there are people. The nature of life lends itself to the experience of grief. Entire spiritual philosophies focus on the reality of life, death, and separation, and the grief that is death's old companion.

Spiritual grounding and religious faith can and do help us get through grief, but it can take a long time. Some never recover from the event, whatever it may be, that triggers the onslaught of overwhelming despair and sadness. A true dream of return can be a powerful antidote for deep grief. There are many dreams in these pages that brought a feeling of peace and resolution to the dreamers. For more thoughts about grief, please see the appendix at the end of the book.

ABOUT THIS BOOK

There are broad differences in the kinds of dreams people get from the other side. The structure of this book reflects those differences. In a majority of dreams, a loved one appears to say a final goodbye, to let those left behind know that everything is fine. Sometimes the living are given a final bit of information or advice. You will find dreams of this kind in Chapter 2.

Chapter 3 offers dreams that inspired and lifted the people who received them. They include dreams where angels appear or the dreamer awakens with a renewed sense of hope, faith, and trust in God. In some of these dreams, the divine reaches out to the dreamer directly. Chapter 4 presents dreams that show how loved ones gone on before still love and watch over us.

Chapter 5 deals with dreams that foreshadow death and let the living know death is approaching. It also talks about how other cultures have viewed life after death. Chapter 6 opens the controversial subject of reincarnation—the idea that we return at some time after we die, in a new and different physical body. In this chapter, you will find personal stories of past lives, dreams, a few famous people who believed in reincarnation, and more.

If you are interested in trying to open communication with the other side, then Chapter 7 may help you make the connection. This chapter contains techniques and advice about how to pierce the veil between the living and the dead. It also looks at some of the ways others have done it over the centuries.

The subject of what happens to us when we die is shrouded in mystery. The dreams and stories you are about to discover offer a glimpse through the veil. What we see on the other side is a different kind of existence, where life continues and we enter a new understanding of who and what we are. Those who have passed through death's door can return to us in our dreams. They bear a message of love we all need to hear.

Chapter 2

.•◆•.

Saying Good-bye

.•◆••◆••◆••◆••◆••◆••◆••◆••◆••◆••◆••◆••◆••◆••◆••◆••◆••◆••◆•.

Ever has it been that love knows not its own depth
Until the hour of separation.

—KAHLIL GIBRAN

S AYING GOOD-BYE to a loved one who is getting ready to die is
one of the hardest things we will ever do. It is hard enough
when we are prepared for the end, worse when death is
unexpected and we have no time to make a final farewell. Even
if we are there with someone at the moment of passing, both the
living who remain and those who move on may not get a chance
to say what is in their hearts. What is it worth to us, the living,
if we get a chance to make that last, loving connection?

The most common dream of return is one in which loved ones
come back to say a final good-bye. Sometimes there wasn't any
time to say good-bye when they were alive. Sometimes they

appear in dreams just before or at the moment of their death. Sometimes they come to comfort the dreamer, days, weeks, or years after they have gone on.

I am often a guest on radio talk shows where people call in with stories, questions, or comments. I hear many dreams and many stories folks want to share. They are true and intimate stories of love and connection from beyond the veil. Some of the most fascinating dreams feature people who die and appear in a dream before anyone knows they are gone. Here is one of those dreams from a radio listener, sent to the host of the show and forwarded on to me.

I Love You

My name is Katherine and I live in Seattle. I recently began listening to your show in the evenings. This past week you had a person on your show talking about nightmares and dreams. I must say I have had very few nightmares but many, many dreams. Near the end of the program, he asked listeners to contact him if they had any dreams involving loved ones that had passed on. Well, here is my short story.

I was about seven years old and my family and I were moving to a new apartment in Kirkland. We moved until late in the evening. Family and friends helped move us all day long.

Late in the evening, it could have been early morning, I awoke from a good but sad experience. Back then, others would have perceived this as a dream, but not me. I viewed it as a visit. It was very clear.

My grandfather and I were standing on the Hood Canal Bridge. Suddenly he moved midway onto the bridge as I was looking at him. Just as I caught up to him, he moved to the other end of the bridge. Again, as I moved, he moved farther, until I found myself upon the rocky edge of the canal. He was fading into the water—without moving his lips, he said, "I love you."

Saying Good-bye

I woke up sobbing, which woke my aunt. I told her that Grandpa died (he is very dear to my heart). She told me, "Go back to sleep, honey, Grandpa is fine. You just had a bad dream."

Moments later, there was a knock at the front door of our apartment. It was the new landlord, asking for my mother. My mother came to the door, and then all I heard was crying—terrible, painful crying. Our phone had not been connected, so my grandmother had called the landlord. My aunt came to my side and said I was right, Grandpa had passed on. No one in my family ever talked about this again until I brought it up recently. My mother never knew. Here I am, thirty-five, and I kept it to myself all these years. Only my aunt and I knew.

This moment changed the rest of my life in many ways. It taught me there is more to life that others were not addressing. It made me search for the truth. As a young child and teen, I did not buy into any one religion. I thought to myself (and sometimes shared with friends) that one person's god is basically the same as another's. This dream inspired me to become a spiritual person.

I don't know if this is the type of information that your guest needed to know. I hope it helps.

Yes, Katherine, that is exactly the kind of information I was looking for. Just a dream, from a seven-year-old who loved her grandpa. How did she know he was dead? No rational explanation will ever be good enough, but the fact remains that Grandpa somehow let her know he was gone and that he loved her.

This visit changed Katherine's life, sparking a lifetime search for spiritual truth. That happens when someone has a dream from the other side. We realize more is going on here than fits within the limits of normal awareness. Once the window opens on knowing there is life after death, it will never close.

The unexpected knock on the door is a frightening possibility for all of us. I work in my community with Victim Services, a team of volunteers that coordinates closely with the police. We undergo intensive training in dealing with the emotional shock and confusion that follows any traumatic incident. Rape, assault, traffic accidents, suicide, shootings, and unexpected death are part of what we address. I have seen firsthand what happens when there is no time to prepare for a loved one's passing. The sudden finality of the event traumatizes those left behind.

It can be very different when the living receive warning in a dream. Then we are somehow prepared for that knock on the door. Here is another story:

I Have to Leave

When my dad died several years back I was living in another state. After emergency surgery (that I knew nothing about) he died quite suddenly of an aneurysm.

Sometime during the night that he died, I had a vivid dream of talking to my dad, and he was saying good-bye. It wasn't a sad dream. In the morning, I woke to someone knocking at my door to give me the news of his death. I opened the door and said, "My dad died last night, didn't he?" The person just stared at me and said, "How did you know?"

I can't explain how I knew, I just did. I have to believe that somehow, some way, my dad found a way to say, "I have to leave now and say good-bye." I might add that the dream was a very peaceful one. It was a floating feeling. I don't ever remember another dream like it before or after. It was a feeling I can't put into words.

People who have true dreams of return or dreams warning of the impending death of someone they love generally say something about the *feeling* of the dream. They comment on how peaceful, or unusual, or different the feeling was from their everyday, normal dreams. That different feeling is a major marker of dreams coming from beyond the veil. One common

42

thread is the sense of incredible love and comfort. Just as in the dream above, the dreamer never forgets the message, nor do other dreams carry the same kind of impact.

It seems that some people who die feel a strong need to find a way to reassure the living. Not everyone has dreams of return. Why do some of us get them, and others not? Perhaps it has to do with the intention of the one who has passed beyond; perhaps it is because the ones left behind have a particular need to know everything is all right. Whatever the reason, the impact is undeniable when a message comes through. Here is another one of those dreams where the living learn someone is gone before the official word is delivered.

Robert's Passing

My husband's brother died in January, of a heart attack, lying on his recliner. His fiancée found him, and she told us he had a peaceful expression, his hands folded, his eyes shut.

The night that Robert died, but before we knew about it, we had some strange experiences. My husband kept hearing the doorbell ring all night. He would go to the door, but no one would be there. This is the only time this happened at that house. He also heard what sounded like bricks falling on the roof of the house.

As I was getting ready for bed and brushing my teeth, I heard Robert's deep, gravelly voice in my ear. It sounded like he was yelling over a bad phone connection. There was a lot of static. "Tell my brother I'm okay, tell Ma I'm okay," he repeated. It really startled me. That night I had a dream.

I found myself in a beautiful garden. Rose bushes and raspberry bushes glowed with an inner golden light . . . it's hard to convey the beauty of this place. A young man approached me. At first I didn't recognize him, then I realized it was Robert. He looked trim, fit, handsome, young—how he must have looked at his physical peak.

He told me, "Tell my brother I'm okay, tell Ma I'm okay, tell everyone I'm okay." There was a glint of amusement in his eye. "Oh, and watch out for the dog poop," he added. Startled, I looked down at my feet. I didn't see any dog poop, but Robert started laughing. "You know, they even let pets in here." I knew he was referring to Bruno, his dog who died a few years back.

"Look, I've got to go. I have to meet some people," Robert said, "but tell everyone I'm okay." I woke from this dream feeling incredibly peaceful.

I shared this dream with Robert's friends and relatives as he instructed, and they shared it with others. At first I was embarrassed about the part with the dog poop. Everyone thought that was typical of Robert. He loved to pull people's legs and get a rise out of them. He thought I was squeamish and liked to kid me.

One of the ways we know someone has returned to us is by things they say and do that are consistent with their real-life personalities. Robert was a kidder, someone who liked to pull people's legs. How perfect that he makes a joke about dog poop, knowing it would activate the dreamer!

It is hard to think of an explanation for the events described other than a successful attempt to communicate from the other side. Remember, the events described here took place before Robert's sister-in-law knew he had died. I know the woman who related these events to me, and I know she is being truthful.

Losing someone you love is difficult; losing more than one person within a brief period is worse. Parents sometimes go within a short period of each other, especially if they are older and have been together a long time. It can be hard for the children left behind to resolve their feelings. Remember Amelia's dream of the hidden love letters in the first chapter? Her parents had an intimate lifetime relationship based on deep love for one another. Here is the rest of her story.

Saying Good-bye

Together Again

My father passed away a year after my mother did. I was desolate at losing the two most important people in my life. I visited the town where I grew up and found myself drawn to our family church, located next door to the Catholic school I had attended through seventh grade. I wandered the halls of the school, then crept into the church and knelt for a brief prayer.

That night, I dreamt I again visited the church, but the doors were locked against me. Sitting on the front steps, I noticed strange movements in a third-floor office at the top of the school, in what used to be the principal's office. When I looked closer, I saw someone fighting off a dove that had found its way indoors. Finally, the dove flew out the window. I watched it fly to the top of the church steeple, where it joined what I knew was a female dove.

In my heart, I heard my father tell me not to grieve. What mattered was that he and my mother were together again. Their love continued beyond the grave.

It would be easy to focus on the psychological content of the symbols in the dream and analyze it from that point of view, but then we might miss the real significance. What is important about this dream is the feeling of comfort and resolution it brought to the dreamer. A dream like this can go a long way toward easing the grief of losing beloved parents. Was it a psychological dream, or did she truly hear her father tell her not to grieve? Does it matter?

Many children never knew one or both of their parents. Accident, war, illness, and misfortune can take a parent away at an early age. But we do not have to remember knowing our parents to have a dream about them returning to us.

Dreams from the Other Side

This Is Not a Dream

When I was in my early twenties, I lived in New York City and had a recurring dream. Every night I dreamed my father had come back from the war. Then I would dream that he told me (in the dream) that this was not a dream. This went on for many nights. I finally decided to visit Germany, and the dreams stopped.

Mind you, I never really knew my father. I was not even a year old when he was reported missing in the war, and during that year he probably saw me twice, when he was home on leave.

I belong to a dream group (the American Association for the Study of Dreams), and after attending their meetings and doing a lot of reading, I almost believe this was a real visitation.

The group she mentions is a serious group dedicated to the study of dreams and dreaming. She almost believes her father visited her. I would say that he certainly did. The same dream repeats itself on different nights. That is worth paying attention to, even if it is "just" a psychological dream. A dream that repeats is a message we need to hear. Notice that the dreams stopped when she decided to visit Germany, where her father died in the war. It is as close as she will ever come to visiting his grave. Does this seem so strange?

I Had No Idea

When I was about thirteen, my step-uncle died. About three months later, I had a dream one night that he came down from heaven and we had a birthday party for him. The next morning I told my mom and stepdad, and they told me that the day before was his birthday, and I had no idea.

Saying Good-bye

This girl did not know it was her step uncle's birthday. Why would she have a dream about her family giving him a birthday party? Because she was the one who was receptive to his message, that's why. It was a way for him to let everyone know that he was all right and wasn't so far away after all.

I Was So Happy He Was There

Two years ago, my eighteen-year-old son took his life. Until this happened, I never really put much thought into life after death. I had my belief that we never die, but no experience to go on.

My son had been gone about a year when I had a visit from him in a dream. In the dream, I was sitting in the front seat of a car with the door open when Travis walked up. I was so overwhelmed and happy to see him, and I ran up to hug him. In life my son was a big teddy bear and loved to give hugs.

I told him I was so happy he was there and hugged him again. I can't remember what was said in the rest of the dream, but we were talking and smiling and I felt so happy. When I woke up, the dream was so real and I felt so good. I still can recall it like I just had it.

Love and healing, hugs and smiles, words of comfort and a reunion with her son. The old cliché about love finding a way was never more appropriate than when applied to these dreams.

It is not only people we love that return to us in dreams. Pets and animals can come back to us as well. Anyone who has truly loved animals knows it is like losing part of yourself when they die. Pets give back unconditional love and they know and respond to love from us. That is their job here, to teach us something about love. I wanted to include at least one dream about a pet returning, and here it is.

Dreams from the Other Side

◆··◆·

The Puppy Looked at Me

I want to submit a very poignant dream from my life. It happened just after I found out my puppy had died. I had already lost my first baby (stillborn) and it really was hard when the puppy died, too.

The dream was different from any other dream I had ever had. I knew in the dream that it wasn't a dream. I was in a light, cloudy type of place and playing with the puppy. We were playing ball and having a wonderful time. Suddenly the puppy looked at me, and I could tell he had to leave, but that it was okay. I was sad but suddenly back in my bed again, and it was over. I felt happy that I got to see him one more time. (He died while I was out of town.)

She knew in the dream that it was not a dream—that is one of the markers of a true dream of return. So is the misty or cloudy setting. So is the feeling of "knowing" that the loved being "has to go." Finally, she awoke feeling happy, because she was able to see him again. Our beloved animal friends survive on the other side, and we will see them again when it is our turn to make the crossing. Love will meet us there.

The Damn Phone Is Always Ringing

My name is Alice. My dad passed away six years ago. Due to my dad's diabetes, he was not aware that his appendix had burst until he became very ill. He was rushed to the hospital, where he suffered a major heart attack.

My family is in California, and I live in Missouri with my husband and little boy, who is three and a half. When I arrived in California, Dad was in a coma and not expected to live. He was hooked up to a life-support machine, which I knew he did not want. We kept him on life support for about four days, until we all decided to take him off and let him pass naturally.

He was heavily drugged with morphine, and I was unable to get a response from him. I stayed with him and spoke, sang, and chanted (prayed). Then one day I went home to rest and that was when he passed. I was so upset. Although I knew it was his time to go, and although I wanted them to pull the plug to honor his wishes, I did not want to let him go. Although I felt we did what was right, I did have a little doubt in my heart. I asked him out loud to please visit me in a dream.

A few weeks passed by and I dreamt of him. In my dream, my dad was a much younger, healthier man. He was in a cabin like the ones you see in a campground. He looked great. I knew in my dream he was dead. I was so excited to talk to him and ask him questions, like how is it on the other side? I asked him if he knew we were thinking about him.

My dad had an incredible sense of humor. He rolled his eyes and showed me a telephone that was ringing constantly. He said he could feel the grieving and it made him feel uncomfortable. I should tell my mother to stop crying because the damn phone was always ringing, and he started to laugh. Then we started to laugh together, because we knew how my mom is. You had to be there, it was funny.

He asked me to please tell my mom to stop crying. He is in a great place and the best thing that anyone can do for the deceased is to offer their prayers. He said that that feels very good and is good for them. He apologized for not squeezing my hand when I held his in the hospital and said he appreciated the songs I sang for him. He tried to acknowledge me but couldn't because he was too tired. He said he wished he had tried harder. I could see in his face that he was very sorry. He hugged me and the love that I felt was so incredibly strong and intense. He said he was proud of me and to take care.

I hope these stories help.

Advances in medical technology have made it all too easy to keep the body alive after the spirit wants to go. Those who remain have to deal with the agonizing decision to turn off the life support. Alice felt a lot better about the family's decision after this dream. I would, too.

Notice that her father passed when she finally went home to rest. That is a common experience. A person who is dying often waits until friends and family have left the room before they let go. Perhaps it is easier, when those who love us are not present. Perhaps those who love us unwittingly hold us back, because they do not want us to go. We wait until they have left before making the journey.

The image of the ringing telephone is a good example of how the dead use dream symbols to make a point. Those who pass on feel the grieving of the living. For Alice's father it was like the constant ringing of a telephone. That is how those on the other side reach us in dreams, through images and symbols we can understand, couched in the language of dreams. The message in this dream is clear: try to let go of the grief and offer prayers for the dead instead of tears. Of course that is easy for dad to say, since he is having quite a different experience than the family left behind! If we really understood the truth of life after death, we would not grieve for long. Nevertheless, it is hard to let go of someone we love, even if we know they live on in a different existence.

FORGIVENESS

It is not unusual for someone to return in a dream and say they are sorry. We have all hurt people we loved, through conscious or unconscious actions. We all have something to regret. Forgiveness is literally good for the soul, whether we are among the living or the dead, whether we are asking for forgiveness or giving it.

Saying Good-bye

Forgiveness is one of the great lessons we are required to learn, along with its intimate companion, love. The interesting thing is that we try to put forgiveness first, when really it is love that makes room for forgiveness. Unconditional love, without judgment of self or other, automatically produces forgiveness. Forgiving becomes a non-issue, because from the viewpoint of unconditional love and non-judgment, there is nothing to forgive. It can be a tough lesson.

She Judged Me Harshly

I lived in a spiritual center for many years The lady who founded the center died at an old age, ninety-seven. I cared for her and helped her in many ways before her departure. At the time, I was married to a man she did not care for. She judged me rather harshly for the union.

About two years after her death she came back to me in a dream and asked me for forgiveness, because she said she "misjudged" me. I took her in my arms and rocked her, and told her I loved her. She went on.

When we cross over, we get a new perspective on whatever we failed to learn here in physical form. Anger, judgment, bitterness, enmity—these human things are mistakes we all make, traps we all fall into. On the other side, there is no judgment, only understanding and compassion, along with guidance and teaching to help us move on in our spiritual development. When we learn the lesson, we might come back to let those we have wronged know we are sorry.

My Ex-Mother-in-Law

My ex-mother-in-law, who was not an ally when she was alive, came back to me in a dream after her death to tell me she really loved me very much. I told her I loved her, too.

Short, sweet, and to the point. I wonder why we find it so difficult to be good to each other while we are here in our physical form? Why do we have to cross over before we understand that love is always a good response? We waste so much time here being angry and judgmental of others, you would think we would have gotten the lesson by now.

We also can have a dream when we feel we are the ones who need forgiveness.

You Never Made Me Unhappy

Thirteen years after my father passed away, I had a dream where I was in a place that felt like the kitchen in the house where I grew up. The kitchen was the room my father spent most of his time in when he was alive. My father was standing in front of me. I told him I thought I had disappointed him throughout his whole life. He looked into my eyes and said, "You never made me unhappy."

The woman who had this dream has an unhappy childhood history and still feels she was to blame for the disastrous relationships of her dysfunctional family. If she can accept the message of the dream, she might change something about how she feels about herself in waking life.

Sometimes it is hard for us to forgive the hurts and frustrations centered in our family experience. The old TV images of happy families where problems are resolved to everyone's satisfaction mirror back to us our wish for a world where understanding moms and dads work things out with their grateful children. In real life, parents make mistakes all the time. This next dream is short but comforted the dreamer.

Saying Good-bye

Arms Full of Flowers

This morning, right before she woke up, my mother had the following dream. I think a bit of history is necessary before I share the dream.

At Thanksgiving of this year, my brother Billy, fifty-four, felt he needed to express his feelings to his parents. Imagine being about sixteen years old and full of anger, blaming your parents for how they have ruined your life. Think of accusing them of broken promises and telling them they were no better than Hitler and Eva Braun, and you have the essence of Billy's communication.

My parents were deeply hurt. After about ten days, my father felt strongly that he did not want there to be a break in the family. He wanted to call Billy to mend things. He said that even if he had to eat crow, he would eat crow. Dad made the call, and although the feelings Billy expressed with me had not changed, they did make peace with each other before Dad died.

Now the dream: My mother is looking for my father. He walks into the room looking really well, with his arms full of flowers. Billy is with him, also with his arms full of flowers. Mom is surprised to see Dad and says, "I thought you were gone." Dad smiles back at her.

In this woman's family, the anger runs deep. Her mother's dream, though, offers an image of healing and forgiveness. It is not just that her husband returns to her, looking well and strong, smiling with love and bearing flowers in his arms. Her estranged son is there as well. He, too, is carrying flowers. Flowers are a gift of love, and in this dream the flowers underscore a message from the other side that healing is both possible and real.

FAMILY REUNIONS

I love the old gospel songs that feature reunion with loved ones on the other side. Classics like "Will the Circle Be Unbroken" by the Carter Family, or the newer "Orphan Girl" by Gillian Welsh, speak to us of what we hope is true. We want to see our loved ones again on the other side of the divide. A radio listener shared this dream of family reunion with me.

You Still Have Things to Do

It was not long after my grandmother died. I always felt a very close bond with her. I didn't get to be there when she died or for her funeral. In the dream, I was walking through a park-type setting. I had to walk around large rocks and gravestones. It was misty, but there was a good feeling there. I saw long rows of tables set up and loaded with food. Relatives that I knew and many that I did not know during this lifetime were standing around visiting.

My grandmother came up to me, hugged me close, and told me I was welcome there. I was so very happy! She looked over at the relatives standing around the tables. "Yes, it's all the family who have passed on," she said. "Someday you will join us, but not yet. You still have things you have to do and must go back."

I was devastated that I could not stay and pleaded with her to let me remain with her. She patted me on the shoulder and said that it was okay, I would be with her someday and not to worry about her.

Suddenly I was back in my bed and woke up. I have never forgotten that dream. It is as clear today as the night I dreamed it. I know this was a visit that actually happened, on some plane we are not aware of during waking hours. There is

54

no doubt in my mind. My grandmother had been around me in spirit a lot during the troubled years of the marriage I was in at that time and comforted me during waking hours also. But those are other stories not related to dreaming. Just thought I would share that with you after hearing you tonight.

The message of this dream for the rest of us is clear. Our families and loved ones still exist on the other side. Perhaps those old spirituals and songs featuring reunion after death are not so far off after all.

You decide for yourself about this next story. Is it a dream, or a waking visit?

You're Dead, You're Not Supposed to Be Here

I had been asleep for several hours, when the doorbell rang. It was midnight. I thought that Brian, my son, must have lost his house key. I went down the stairs to let him in. I opened the door expecting to see Brian and was shocked to see both my parents standing in the doorway.

They stepped inside into the hall. I asked, "What are you doing here? You're dead, you're not supposed to be here." My father answered. "We had to come, I could not let your mother come alone." I asked again, "Why are you here?"

"To make sure you are all right."

I assured them I was fine. They both looked so young and happy! My mom never spoke one word. She did have the most wonderful smile on her face—it was warm; she seemed to shine. We embraced and kissed to say good-bye. I could feel her warm body, her energy. It may sound strange, I know.

They both turned and walked out the door. I started back up the stairs.

The next morning I awoke feeling absolutely wonderful, happy, with many emotions. I had no memory of what had happened hours earlier. Later that day, as I was cleaning the mirror in my bedroom, it all came rushing back with every detail and the most wonderful feeling of pure joy.

She called her five sisters and four brothers after the dream to tell them of the visit. It brought joy and memories of good times to all of them. Such a dream touches everyone in a family, regardless of who dreams it.

All dreams from the other side bear witness to our innate psychic abilities. We are psychic beings who have forgotten how to apply our natural gifts. "Psychic" is one of those words we view with suspicion, part of a legacy left over from the days of darkness and ignorance that fill much of human history.

Some people are more sensitive than others, more attuned to their surroundings than the majority, and more inclined to receive images and messages from the other side. Often I will hear stories from dreamers that others in their family have had similar experiences. Sometimes the ability to receive these kinds of dreams seems to pass down from mother to daughter, father to son. The next dream comes from a woman who is a vivid and psychic dreamer.

My Mother's Dream

My family are Polish survivors of World War II. Although not Jewish, their stories of horror are similar. In 1939, my mother was in a hospital in Slonim, which is now in Belarus. She had contracted meningitis. Her mother (my grandmother) stopped visiting the hospital when the Russians invaded and began deporting Poles living in the region.

The Russians sent my grandmother to a Siberian work camp, where she died within the year. My mother was fourteen or so at the time, we're not certain of her age. She recuperated with kindly friends of the family for a year or so, until they, too, were sent to Siberia. During this year of recovery, she had the following dream.

Saying Good-bye

*My mother woke to see my grandmother standing at the foot
of her bed, wearing a nightgown with flowers on it. She came
to say good-bye to her daughter, having been very worried about
her, to ask about her health, and to tell her she loved her. My
mother awoke in fear.*

*When the Russians joined the allies, my mother was able to
make her way out of Siberia. She ultimately arrived in
England at the end of the war. She was out of touch with her
siblings until the 1950s. Via letters, she was able to confirm
the details of my grandmother's death, including a description
of the nightclothes she was wearing when she died. They were
the same as the ones in the dream. She also confirmed that my
grandmother had been very concerned about my mother at the
time that she died.*

Only a deep love can reach across time and space at the
moment of death to say good-bye. Like the dreams at the beginning of this chapter, they show how our connection to the ones
we love reaches past the veil.

I Prayed to Mom to Help Me Rest

*Several months after everything had settled down after Mom's
passing, I was back in Colorado. I was in a numb state of dis-
belief, not getting much sleep, and thinking of Mom constantly.
One sleepless night I silently prayed to Mom to help me rest. I
couldn't sleep on my own, and I was missing her so much.*

*That night she came to me in my dream. It was as if I could
hear her and touch her and see her so clearly. In the dream, I
was sitting at my desk at work and she walked through the
door, younger in years and beautifully vibrant with health and
youth. She was happy and smiling and told me she was fine
and that everything was all right. I woke up that morning
having rested better than ever with an incredible healing experience from Mom.*

Dreams from the Other Side

In many dreams of return, the one who is gone appears healthy, full of energy, and better than they may ever have looked in life. We return to health and well-being after we die, if we are to judge by all of the dreams that show this kind of radiant, personal renewal.

One thing I notice about these dreams is that the annoying or uncomfortable habits of the people we knew do not seem to be present on the other side. For some of us with difficult families, that might be a good thing! It can be a real challenge to get along with someone we have to put up with because they are "family." Hard times can make for hard people. Here is a dream that reminds us that everyone can use a little love.

A Special Bond

I had this dream about my deceased uncle a few days after his death. My uncle was sixteen when World War II broke out. Captured by the Germans in 1939, he was forced to work in a German labor camp for the duration of the war. He was a troubled man who few people knew, or cared to get to know. I was born in the 1950s, and for whatever reason, I sensed something about him that few people did. I loved him deeply, although there was much about him that was unlovable. To this day, his daughter, my cousin, harbors little but resentment toward him. But he and I had a special bond.

I was in a misty room, bluish gray, with nothing distinct about it. I wasn't frightened, but the room seemed very real to me. It seemed more real than everyday life. I wondered if I was awake or sleeping. Then my uncle walked into view. He died of cancer and in great pain, so I was concerned and wanted to know how he was feeling. He told me that he was fine. He ignored the small talk and told me he loved me. I said I loved him as well. He embraced me in a bear hug. I was surprised at his strength. Then I woke up.

Saying Good-bye

An interesting dream about a difficult man, who was loved and came back to affirm that love. The misty room is similar to other dream settings where a loved one comes back with a final message or good-bye. There is a strong feeling of reality even when the setting is neither familiar nor clearly defined. A misty room, a misty light, a place where the boundaries of the scene blur into nothingness—these are familiar to many dreamers.

The woman who had this dream about her uncle had another dream about him just a few months later. Remember, this troubled man left behind a legacy of mixed feelings, especially for his daughter, the dreamer's cousin.

I'm Fine

My cousin, although conflicted about her father, was very sad about his death. He was on her mind a great deal, although I did not know it. I live a few hundred kilometers away, and we don't see each other often.

In my dream, there were many people in a room. They were milling about. My cousin was there, fussing over a baby sitting on a couch. The baby was content, but my cousin would not stop her ministrations. She just could not settle down. The baby turned to me and I realized that it was my uncle. He told me to tell my cousin that he really didn't need to be taken care of, that he was fine.

I called my cousin the following day. She was deeply moved by this message, breaking into tears. She really needed to hear that her father was okay and that he didn't want her to worry about him anymore.

This is a very symbolic dream, a good example of how the dead use the vehicle of our dreaming consciousness to get a message across, expressing it through our inner dream language. The baby is fine but the cousin cannot stop fussing over him. In the dream, the dreamer recognizes that the baby is really her dead uncle. The baby tells the dreamer to let the cousin know that everything is okay. The dreamer, who knows she gets good information in her dreams, calls up her cousin with the message. She only then finds out that the dead man's daughter has been worrying about her father for months and is deeply relieved to hear the message of the dream.

It is also possible that the dreamer unconsciously picked up cues from her cousin indicating unexpressed worry and concern about her cousin's deceased father. She could then have had a regular, psychological dream prompting her to call her cousin and offer the message of comfort. In that case, we need no visit from the other side to explain the dream. What do you think?

Don't You Miss Us?

I read your article on dreaming of loved ones that have passed over. My mother passed away about six months ago. She had been in the hospital but had picked up, and we were hopeful that she would be okay. The day before she passed away, she was laughing and chatting with everyone. That night, I could not sleep, and I kept thinking that all she needed was one bad night and she might not make it. Early the next morning, I received the phone call to come to the hospital, but when I got there, she was gone.

I am from a very close family and we were all especially close to Mum. I have had a few dreams about Mum. About three weeks ago, I had a different type of dream. I dreamt I was talking to her from the other side. Although I could not see her, I knew it was her in my dream. I dreamt she was talking. I did not hear what she said at first, but I can remember saying to her, "But don't you miss us, Mum?" She then said, "Of course I do." Then I asked her if she was happy, and she said, "Yes." I then woke up.

I think it has helped me over the last few weeks, even though I still grieve for her.

Saying Good-bye

The theme I see repeated over and over when talking with dreamers is one where uncertainty is resolved by contact in a dream with someone who has gone. We need to know our loved ones are all right, that they are happy and at peace, and that their troubles are no longer of concern.

A powerful dream of return can help us confront our own fears of death. It's hard to hang on to fear if we get a real feeling for the reality of life after death. These dreams can also provide genuine resolution for feelings of loss and grief, but I am sure that there is more to the story than just psychological adjustment. How else can we explain some of the dreams in this book where information is given that could not possibly be known to the dreamer, or warnings issued that are borne out in waking life?

Parents show up more than anyone else in dreams of return. That makes sense, since most of us will outlive our parents in the natural order of things. Of all the relationships we will have in our lives, the one with our parents is the most fundamental and perhaps the most complex. It is a mixed bag of emotions, and love is always a factor.

Sometimes a dream of return is long and full of imagery; sometimes it is short and direct, a simple statement that brings completion and a sense that all is well. What counts is the feeling of the dream, the sense for the dreamer of reconnection to the one who is gone. This next dreamer was very upset with her father's passing. She is a psychologist, well aware of the way our human minds can compensate for deep feelings of grief. She is convinced her father really did return to her in this dream. It has helped her come to terms with his death.

Everything Is Fine

My dream was this—I was in the kitchen at the sink and my father was sitting up on the butcher-block counter. He said to me, "Everything is fine, honey."
It was such a relief. It was within two weeks of his death.

How you feel in the dream, the kind of setting, and the actions all tell you something. A true dream of return can bring deep feelings of resolution, like this next example. The dreamer has tried to describe the setting and feeling as if writing a story. His dream came to him five nights after his father died.

Into the Lake

Sitting on a large volcanic rock outcropping that ran into a small, gorgeous, Colorado mountain lake, I absorbed the view and sensations. Beautiful, diamondlike sparkles, reflecting from the sun, danced upon the crests of the small waves. A warm breeze blew in my face and ruffled my hair. I felt peaceful and glad to be in the mountains that I love. As I looked up, the beautiful fall colors of aspen trees shimmered and glittered as they danced and flapped in the wind. Overhead I saw a cloudless, calming, deep blue Colorado sky.

A breeze flapped my shirt and blew over my body. It felt like the warmth I have known in my life, yet at the same moment it seemed to be a deeper warmth, more than I had ever felt before. It went around my body, through my body, and into my soul. My body seemed to recognize this penetrating, calming, radiating, familiar warmth from long ago.

I looked to my left and saw Dad sitting on the same rock outcropping, just out of my physical reach and higher up. I was surprised he did not look like the sixty-year-old I had known him to be. He looked much younger, as if he were in the prime of his life, about twenty-five. His gray hair and beard were gone. His hair blew in the wind. He was wearing an old-fashioned black bathing suit.

In life, I do not have many memories of him wearing bathing suits. This one reminded me of one I saw him wearing in an old picture, when he was a young man in the air force.

He often told me how he had the time of his life during his

*assignment overseas in Athens. Dad told me stories of living in
a villa within sight of the Parthenon. He kept large vats of
Greek wine on hand for all occasions. He went sailing, scuba
diving for treasure, hunting for pheasant, and motorcycling.*

*As he sat on the rock smiling, I noticed he had less chest hair,
like when he was younger; the gray was gone. He was thinner,
looking young and vigorous, if not somewhat mischievous. His
smile turned into the biggest grin. His teeth were perfect. They
were brilliant and somewhat blinding (in life his teeth were
bad and many were false). Dad's teeth sparkled like ones you
would see in a television ad. His eyes were the clearest I have
ever seen them—they gleamed and radiated pure joy. I felt a
lot of love coming from him.*

*As I turned to take in the lake, I thought to myself or said
to him, "I'm really sorry we did not spend more time together
and have more adventures. I greatly enjoyed the adventures we
had when I was young." He replied, "Me, too." I thought for
awhile and then said, "I always wanted to try scuba diving."
He replied with a sincere but mischievous look, "Me, too." He
grinned. Suddenly I was falling into the water. As I was
falling, I noticed he was falling into the water, too. Oddly for
a Colorado mountain lake, the water felt warm. Under the
water, I found myself suddenly in a wet suit and scuba gear. So
was Dad. We began to swim.*

This is a dream we could see as psychological, rather than as
a true dream of return. In that case, we would interpret the dive
into the lake as a plunge into the unconscious. The dream would
present a symbolic journey of discovery about the dreamer and
his father.

Perhaps—but there are other distinguishing elements to this
dream that tip the assessment toward the other side. One element is the intensity of warmth and good feeling in the dream.
By now, you know this is a common characteristic of dreams
from beyond, although other kinds of dreams may also have this

quality. Another is the physical appearance of the father. The gray hair is gone, the infirmities of physical life no longer present, the eyes clear and full of joy.

The dreamer sees his father as he appeared in the time when he was most happy. Young, vibrant, happy about his life in a beautiful city in the beautiful land of Greece, wearing the kind of bathing suit we see in old photos.

HEALING ON THE OTHER SIDE

This change to the look of youth, vibrancy, and physical well-being is a common marker of true dreams of return. Some people who have a near-death experience see friends, loved ones, or relatives restored to youth and beauty, waiting for them on the other side. When we die our spirit takes on a different form, one not subject to the pains and limitations of our physical world.

It is not possible for us to fully understand what that means, because we are still here, still in physical form, and still experiencing the weaknesses, ills, and limitations of the body. Anyone who has had a near-death experience or an out-of-body experience can tell you that it is true. When the soul lifts away from the form, the burdens of the form fall away.

I have heard stories of people with near-death experiences who found themselves whole and well for the time they spent on the other side and out of their body. Amputees report they were whole; the blind see; pain ceases. All the infirmities come back when the soul reenters the body after the experience. That is one reason some people have such a difficult time after a near-death experience. They have to return to the body they knew, but now know that there is a different reality where pain and limitation imposed by form do not exist.

Here is a dream offering a glimpse of the healing that takes place on the other side.

Saying Good-bye

My Cousin Jimmy

Jimmy was two years my junior and my brother's best buddy. In life, Jimmy had a funny, vibrant, and incredibly witty personality. But he had a host of health problems. He was born with idiosyncratic scoliosis and was severely deformed. Through the course of his twenty-three years, he had over 150 surgeries, eighteen in the first year of his life. He reached a maximum height of three-foot-five, had a funny grating voice, and couldn't do much physically because of the limitations of his lung capacity. He did have a joy for life that went totally beyond his physical limitations and inspired everyone who could look past his physical presence and get to know him.

He died at age twenty-three due to various complications from the shunt that drained fluid from his brain. About a year after he died, I dreamt that I was traveling in Vietnam. I have traveled extensively, but never to Vietnam, nor do I have any desire to visit Vietnam. Nonetheless, that is where I was, and that is where I found Jimmy. I almost didn't recognize him. He was "perfect." His body was not stunted, twisted, short, bent, or crippled in any way. He was physically beautiful.

He was in a bar enjoying a cigar, a drink, and the company of several beautiful Vietnamese women who clearly adored him. When he saw me, a smile broke across his face, then a look of worry. He said, "Hello! Nice to see you here." We talked for awhile and I saw that he was completely happy. I still hadn't realized I was dreaming, it all seemed so real. As we were saying our good-byes, I said, "I can't wait to tell everyone you're here, they'll be so happy to know where you are!" He said, "No, please don't tell anyone I'm here. I'm happy and I don't want to go back." I agreed, but I was still confused.

Then I woke up and realized it was all a dream. At first I was sad as I remembered Jimmy was gone. Then I realized he was happy that he was "normal" and wanted to be remembered that way, not as just a beautiful soul trapped in a physically deformed body.

It would be hard to create a better contrast to Jimmy's earthly reality of deformity and physical challenge than the picture in this dream. A cigar, a drink, beautiful women, and an exotic country are all things Jimmy never was able to experience or enjoy. On the other side, all things are possible.

We may get a message from someone who has passed on about something left behind—like the love letters hidden in the attic. We might get a message about a different kind of legacy as well. Sometimes we need to take a hard look at our life and some gentle prompting from the other side can get us thinking in new and positive ways. The dead are not allowed to solve our problems for us, but there isn't any rule against subtle guidance. Healing means more than physical health and well-being. Healing can be of another sort as well.

You Have Something of Mine

I have dreamt many times of my parents since their deaths. They look healthy and happy, as if the afterlife is better for them. It is so good to see them that I am sad when I wake up and realize it was only a dream. My dad is usually silent, but walking tall and smiling, and I get the feeling that he is proud of me.

I can only remember a couple of dreams where he spoke, but I cannot remember what he said. Mom always talks to me. She is playful and silly just as when she was alive, but lacks the spaceyness she was known for in this life.

Several years ago, I went through a phase where I was dreaming about my parents almost every night. They were both in my dreams, but Mom was featured more than Dad. One night, I was sitting at a table in a hospital cafeteria talking to my mom. In my dream, it was a beautiful day and sunlight was streaming in through the ground-floor windows, even though there was a lot of shrubbery to block it. I remember noticing that Mom was dressed a lot like she was in a picture I have of her, and I said, "Mom, how is it that you manage to come back from the dead so often?" Her reply was, "Because you have something of mine and I want to help you figure out what to do with it."

I don't remember the exact conversation after that, but I realized she wanted me to figure out for myself what it was. After that, the nightly dreams of my parents stopped and I didn't have any dreams of either of them for quite a while (that I remember). It took me a long time to figure out what I had that was hers. Eventually I decided it was her bitterness. She had been dealt too many cheap shots in life. So have I. Both of us tend to get angry about it even though nothing can change the past.

Since that time I have worked at finding less destructive ways to think of what has happened in my life, as well as consciously choosing not to be around certain kinds of people. I don't think I would have realized it was something I needed to do had I not had that dream of Mom in the cafeteria.

On the other side, everything becomes a lot clearer. We can understand and learn from the mistakes made when we were in physical form. For this dreamer, it looks like Mom is trying to help her daughter get the lesson in this life, so she can move on. That is a healing process for both of them.

You never know who is going to show up in a dream from the other side. It may be someone you would least expect.

You Are Dead, This Is Crazy

When I was in high school, I dated a guy for several years. He was the greatest love of my life, and we dated off and on through college. The last time I spoke to him, we got in a big fight and I threw him out of my house. We never spoke again.

Dreams from the Other Side

A few years later, he died a sudden, unexpected death. Shortly after his death, I dreamed of him showing up at my house. I kept telling him, "You are dead, this is crazy." In my dream, we sat and talked for hours about what had happened in my life since I had spoken to him. I told him details about school, my niece, and specific things that were going on in my life. He was smiling and laughing. The dream felt like it lasted forever.

The dream ended with me telling him to come over again. He said he would. Since then, he does pop up in my dreams on occasion. We just talk and visit. During the time he died, I was seriously involved with someone else. I was twenty-two and in college. I was deeply affected by his death, and after that dream, I woke up feeling so close to him and calm. It really gave me closure and a good feeling. It also made me miss him greatly.

Whatever they fought about, it wasn't enough to end the love between them. Now they have a peaceful friendship that survives beyond the grave. I would call it friendship, wouldn't you? When you can sit down with someone, laugh, and share the things of your life, that's friendship. Whether in a dream or in real life, the result is the same.

Resolution is a major theme in dreams of the dead. Aside from our desire to know that all is well with them, wherever they are and in whatever existence they now have, we want resolution for our feelings of loss and grief. A dream of return can be worth years of grief therapy and can dramatically speed the healing process or even bring it to completion. Most of all, we feel our beloved is still with us somehow. It's true—they are never really gone.

We Just Hugged Forever

My brother, Jonathan, was killed in a car accident two years ago, June 5. I never really had any dreams about him or anything until this past year. Finally, one night I had a dream about him.

68

Saying Good-bye

I was with my mom in our living room near the record player/stereo. I think we might have been talking about Jonathan, and all of a sudden he appeared. I said, "Jonathan, you're here with us again." We just hugged forever and it felt so good to hold him close in my arms. It was as if we never let go. I don't really remember how it ended, but we just hugged forever. It was so nice . . . I will always remember that feeling. It was a very inspiring dream.

When I look at this dream I can really feel her joy at seeing her brother again. It almost makes me want to cry! It is truly a dream of completion. That feeling of hugging her lost brother will stay with her all of her life, and it will continue to bring her comfort when she thinks of him.

Life can produce sad and tragic surprises. Accidents that take our loved ones from us are especially traumatic. One moment the people we love are with us, the next gone, and we have no warning, no time to prepare. We are angry, grief stricken, bewildered. A dream that brings the survivor peace of mind is priceless, a real gift from beyond the veil.

Sharon's Dream

I have no doubt my mother visited me in a dream after she and six other members of my family were killed in an accident, a poisonous gas leak in West Texas. I was tortured by images of their deaths. They awakened and tried to get out, only to watch each other die, one by one.

In my dream, I was sitting in my mother's kitchen, dreaming in color! She came around the room divider from the living room to the kitchen, glowing. I began to tell her how happy I was to see her and asked where she had been. She told me she was not back to stay, that she only came to tell me she was okay, happy, and where she wanted to be.

I miss my mother more as I grow older and wiser, but my memory of her is from the dream, not the tragic ending. I love you, Mother!

This dream has one of the markers indicating a true dream of return. Some of us dream mostly in black and white; some of us dream mostly in color. Sharon always dreams in black and white, but this time her mother appears in vivid color. When we see a dramatic change like this in a dream, from black and white to color, we know the dream is special, deserving careful attention. If we already dream in color, then an unusual dream may present itself in especially vivid, electric colors, almost hallucinogenic in nature. Things glow; they radiate light. The dream leaves a sense of intensity and magic with our waking mind.

I can only imagine Sharon's torment, thinking about how her family died in this awful accident. Because of the dream, though, she laid to rest the painful images of their deaths. She tuned in instead to an image of love and peace, a feeling that her mother is fine and well. I call that a healing dream.

I'm Okay, Grandma

I understand you are writing another book, and you are asking people to submit something that has occurred to them in their dreams. My first grandson died at twenty-two months of age after a long illness with a bad heart. He and I seemed to have a very special relationship, perhaps even on a higher level than my daughter. When he died, a part of me seemed to die.

Shortly after his death, he appeared to me, standing up in his coffin, waving, saying, "I'm okay, Grandma, I'm okay." After that, I was able to say good-bye to him. It scared me very much; I awoke startled, but then I surmised he was telling me it was time to get on with my life.

Thank you for letting me share this experience with you.

And thank you, for sharing this experience with us.

Dreams of good-bye can bring an end to grief. When personal loss throws our life into turmoil, it takes time and patience to allow things to realign themselves with the new reality. There is no standard timetable for healing. That is the first thing to know about handling grief. The following dream is a good example of what I mean.

I Never Allowed Myself to Mourn

When I was seven, a woman came to me in a dream and told me that my mother was going away, but that I would be fine. The morning I woke from the dream, I kept crying so hard my mother finally had to drag it out of me . . . she cried with me, because she knew I had told her future. I lost her to cancer when I was ten.

When I was twenty-six, I had a dream of a doctor trying to convince me that my mother was dead. I replied, "Yes, I know this," several times. We began to walk down a corridor, as he continued to tell me she was dead.

We walked into a room and I saw my mother's body lying on a gurney. I turned to look at my mother's body, lying in this all-white room. Her body slowly began to move. I spoke to her, saying, "But, Mom, you're dead," and she replied, "Yes, honey, I know." She chuckled and rose. She got off the gurney and came over to hug me, reassuring me that yes, she knew she was dead.

I had never allowed myself, in all of that time, to mourn my mother's passing. Not until she came and helped me understand, in that dream.

For this woman, it took nineteen years before she could face the reality of her feelings, and it took the return of her mother in a dream to do it.

FRIENDS AND LOVERS

Friendship can carry as strong a bond as family, and our good friends may return to us in our dreams. Most of the dreams people have about friends and lovers who have gone on bring a sense of completion and closure to the dreamer. They usually signal the final encounter with the beloved.

Sometimes these dreams are detailed and complex, sometimes short and direct like this next one. The length of the dream doesn't matter, just the feeling of it.

Good-bye to an Old Friend

I walk out the front door of my parents' house on a warm day and look over to see Dorothy in front of her house, checking the mail by the front steps. I am glad to see her and call hello.

I know she is dead these past couple of weeks, but I am very glad to see her. She seems real and solid. I walk over to visit her. I am directly in front of the porch steps, saying good-bye to Dorothy.

"Are you in pain?" I ask.

"No," she replies, shaking her head.

We say good-bye with a big, warm hug. It feels sweet and uplifting and genuine. Good-bye, Dorothy. Good-bye, old friend!

Hugs again, and that same feeling—a sense of love, connection, and, more than anything else, a sense of genuineness. It is no different for the dreamer than if his friend was standing right there. In fact, she was, in a meaningful and real way.

Love is the underlying theme in all dreams of return. Love is something we can never really lose. We may move through different relationships and times in our life, but we never forget love, even if we never see the loved one again.

Saying Good-bye

Sometimes death takes someone out of our lives, and we cannot understand why. We don't know why life had to end for the one we loved. Then, sometimes, we get a dream that helps us understand.

I Had to Go

I had a boyfriend whom I loved dearly. We had grown up knowing and loving each other since about age eight. He lived in Indiana. I moved to Colorado with my family at about age twelve. Billy and I stayed in touch and in love over the years, although we had other relationships. We thought we would marry one another one day.

Away at college, I received a call that Billy had died in a drowning accident while training with the Navy SEALs. I was crushed, of course. Sometime not long after his passing, I had a dream in which he came to me.

The dream: I was at the lake where we lived when I was eleven, in Michigan. Billy came to me in the water. We were in shallow water by the shore and were under the water. He told me this was how he had died, under the water, drowning. I asked him why and told him how upset I was. He told me he was so sorry, but he had to go. He told me he was okay and that he loved me and would always love me, and again that he was sorry he'd had to go.

That was the end. I remember the love and knowing he is okay and that was his path, what he had to do.

Some of us lose more than our share of friends. I know the woman who had the dream above. Linda is a caring and outgoing person, the kind of person who allows many people into her life. Over the years, many she knew have crossed over. Here is another dream of hers. I think her friends return to her because of her genuine concern and feeling for them.

Dreams from the Other Side

I Felt Such Joy

I had a very close male friend in high school. I loved him dearly. Sometime in my early twenties, I lost track of him and could not find him. I knew he was in New York but never knew how to contact him. When I actually did live in New York, I hesitated to really try to look him up. I never quite understood why. In retrospect, perhaps I knew on some level that he was ill and I was not up to facing it.

I often dreamed I was looking for him. I longed for him in my dreams and could not find him. I searched for him in my dreams, dream after dream, and could not find him. Some time after I moved back to Colorado, I had a dream in which my friend came to me. I was so happy to see him. He looked great. He was dressed up in a suit. I told him I had been looking for him for so long and how I had missed him. He told me he was doing well and that he loved me and had missed me, too. We hugged each other. I felt such joy and relief at finally finding him.

On Christmas Eve about a year later, I went to our old church where my friend and I had been in youth group and choir together. My husband and I were talking to the minister there, and the subject of my friend's mother came up. He told us she had lost a son. When I asked who, he said it had been my friend. He died about the same time I had the dream in which he came to see me.

Since then, I have had a number of dreams where this friend visits me. We talk. We talk about him having had AIDS and that he is well and happy now. I often hug and kiss him in the dreams. I always know in the dream that he is "dead," and that he is well and not contagious. We share a deep and ful-filling love and connection. I appreciate that he comes to visit me like he does.

Saying Good-bye

AIDS is one of the great plagues of all time. On the other side, it does not exist. That alone is a message worth hearing about.

Linda has active dream relationships with her friends. I don't think these are psychological dreams, although she has told me some dreams that fall into that category. The difference is in the feeling of the dreams.

Dreams of good-bye, in a way, confirm the opposite—there is no real good-bye, only a time, for a while, when we are separated from family and friends. When someone returns in a dream to tell us good-bye, it is an affirmation of ongoing life. They are gone in the physical form, but on a different plane of existence they are still here.

Good-bye dreams allow us to let the other go. Perhaps you have had the experience of saying goodbye to someone who is about to go off on a long journey, or who is moving away to a distant place. We know when these changes occur that we might never see that person again in this life. We feel sad, but it never occurs to us to try and hang on. They have to go, and only time will reveal whether we will see them again, and when.

Good-bye dreams are a way of seeing our loved ones off on a long journey. We can let them go, knowing that we may someday see them again. If you have one of these dreams about people you love, bless them on their journey and let them go. Soon enough, you will be together again.

Chapter 3

·-•-··-•-··-•-··-•-··-•-··-•-··-•-··-•-··-•-··-•-··-•-··-•-··-•-·

Messengers of Love

·-•-··-•-··-•-··-•-··-•-··-•-··-•-··-•-··-•-··-•-··-•-··-•-··-•-·

The best and most beautiful things in the world
Cannot be seen, nor even touched, but are felt in the heart.
—HELEN KELLER

NGELS. Who among us would not want to see an angel? Perhaps we have, even if we are not talking about a beautiful and radiant being with wings. Anyone who has seen or felt an angel's presence has no difficulty believing in the reality of divine messengers. Angels are messengers from the divine, and the message they bring is one of love and support.

Angels come in many different shapes and forms. The Judaic tradition, for example, describes an elaborate hierarchy of heavenly and angelic beings that is prominent in both Christian and Islamic thinking. How an angel looks to us seems to depend on our cultural background. To someone from one of the three major Western religions, angels look like the images we are familiar with from religious art. To someone from the East, the appearance may be different, but the essence is the same. When an angel appears, we see what we are conditioned to see.

A manifestation of the divine could frighten us. It makes sense to present an image we are familiar with and can understand. Confronted with the full face of God, we would be overwhelmed.

There is a great epic poem in the East called the *Bhagavad Gita* ("Song of God") that illustrates this point. One of the core teachings of Hinduism, the *Gita* tells a story of war, love, and the way to God. In the story, the main character is prince Arjuna. Arjuna is a great warrior. Krishna, who is actually God in human form, is his charioteer. Throughout the poem, Krishna instructs and guides Arjuna, helping him understand right action and behavior. He teaches Arjuna how to reconcile his human confusion with the clarity of the divine plan.

At one point in the story, Arjuna begs Krishna to show him his true self. He wants to see God in all his glory. Krishna tells Arjuna that it would be too much, but Arjuna insists. For just an instant, Krishna reveals his full form to Arjuna, who is overwhelmed by the sight. Even this great warrior, who fears nothing except acting without honor, falls to his knees in terror at the sight of God. How would you and I respond?

An angel doesn't have to look like one of the paintings we have all seen. An angel can look like you and me. That is one premise of the popular television show *Touched by an Angel*. The angels look just like people, until the moment of revelation when they let us know they are divine beings. You may have met an angel but did not know it. There isn't any rule that says angels have to appear in full regalia: wings, robes, and all. If you think about your life, perhaps you can remember a time or times when something or someone intervened to avert disaster or sorrow. Perhaps *you* have been touched by an angel.

When I was eight years old, I almost drowned. I was attending one of those daily summer camp programs popular in the 1940s. At the time, I lived in Philadelphia, where the program was run by the Young Men's Christian Association. The YMCA had a huge pool and one of the daily camp activities was swimming time.

Things were a *lot* different in the '40s in terms of how kids were supervised and what kinds of safety protocols were followed. The pool was tiled all around, something that would never happen now because of the danger of slipping and falling on the wet tiles. The program had many children of varying ages, at least a hundred or so boys from ages seven and eight up to twelve years old. All of these children would run naked and screaming, full tilt boogie, at the pool, piling off the diving board and jumping like mad frogs into the water.

One day I dove off the board and as I hit the water someone jumped after me and kicked me hard in the back of the head. I went down like a stone in twelve feet of water. I remember looking at the drain in the bottom of the pool. I was choking for an instant, and then I stopped fighting the water and felt it fill my lungs. I was breathing the water, which is not a good idea. I was just drifting there, feeling wonderfully peaceful, when someone grabbed me and pulled me to the surface and then onto the floor at the side of the pool.

I never saw who it was—it wasn't the lifeguard, who seemed conspicuously absent. All I saw was a pair of legs walking away as I began coughing up and choking on the water I had been blissfully breathing just seconds before. No one paid any attention.

I know I was saved by an angel. There are other possible explanations, but the feeling of that rescue was one I have never forgotten. Like the dreams from the other side, the feeling of the divine is one of the markers telling you of an angelic encounter. Even at eight years old, I knew something was different about that particular event.

Angels have become a popular subject in the last several

years. Why is that happening? Because people have miraculous and powerful experiences, including visions and dreams of angels, where real results manifest in their lives. It is happening because the doorway to the other side is open when needed. Angels bring us both real assistance and a renewal of hope. They bring a breath and scent of the divine.

If we lose faith and hope, the light goes out of the day. Even when we hold strong religious or spiritual beliefs, the shocks of life can upset our sense of connection to spirit and cause us to shut down. It is one thing to believe God exists and that all will be well if we just have faith. It's another if we get a real feeling for it. Angels, whether they stand before us or appear in dreams, give us the feeling of the presence of God.

We make many mistakes during our journey here on Earth. We act unconsciously, foolishly, until an awakening sense of spirit and compassion helps us stop behaving like selfish children. A dream from the other side can lift us and set us on a new course of service and love, with the recognition that we are not alone. We all have spiritual and angelic guides to help us along the way.

A Little Gold Box in the Center of Myself

I was looking up to the sky, looking for something, and I dreamed I felt very sad about my life. In the waking world, I was.

I was staring at the night sky full of stars, no moon, when an angelic being appeared out of nowhere. It said to me, "You can have one wish, to ask about everything around you, even things you don't know are real. What is your wish?" I remember wishing and saying, "My only wish is to know if God and angels really exist and have been there in my life." The angel spoke and told me, "So be it, here is your answer." The angel disappeared and another being was present, without form. It was pure light, and the feeling I got was pure light, love, and peace. This being, this light, put what seemed to be a hand to the left side of my face, and another hand to my right side, just below my arms.

It lifted me in midair and cradled me like a baby in its mother's arms. The light surrounded me. I felt no physical body, no burdens, no pain, no hurtful memories, no stress, only a tremendous amount of purity, love, and peace. I started to cry for this feeling, it was so big and huge I couldn't describe it. It felt so good to be at peace within my soul. I wept for joy and sadness, because I knew it would not last, though I wanted it to last forever and wanted to stay there forever, for eternity.

Then I was slowly let down to the ground. All I could do in the dream was sit on my knees and not feel or think—just be in awe and try to remember the brief moment of whatever it was I had experienced.

My dream ended with me sobbing on the ground because it was gone from me and I was in my physical body again. I woke up crying because the feeling stayed with me. I felt it in my bones, my flesh, my heart, but most of all my soul. I cried for fifteen minutes, wanting so badly to have it back, to keep it in a little gold box in the center of myself.

What the feeling came from, I don't know. I like to believe it was God, but I guess I'm just not meant to know for sure. I still go back to that dream in my mind and relive the feeling and the dream. This dream made me see that someone is listening to my cries, even if I don't know who that is.

I am learning to repair the damage my life has done to my spirit and my heart. I have confidence now that someone is hearing my cries each time I tear myself down to repair myself. "You have to clear out the old to make way for the new and better." My father told me that recently, and I never knew what it meant until now.

One true marker of a real dream from the other side is that it produces change. A change of heart, a change of mind, a change in the way we view things. Anyone who touches spirit in such a dream keeps the memory forever, written indelibly on the heart.

This young woman has had a difficult time and is struggling with the forces within that led her in the wrong direction. Her dream gives her strength and helps her get through the day, one day at a time.

Sometimes a dream of God and angels may leave us with a sense of loss, a feeling of something touched but not possessed. That's okay—it still urges us on and inspires us to seek out other ways to make the feelings real in our waking life. Here is an example.

A Ladder to Heaven

Here is a dream from many years back that had a powerful feeling of God for me. I am climbing a ladder to heaven at an immeasurable height above the ground and entering the clouds. The ladder seems weak and sways back and forth. Eventually I reach a height above the clouds, when a "golden light" hits me with an extreme intensity. It is more than light; it carries with it the sum of all human emotion, the powerful sum of all life in the universe. I shudder as it fills me.

It is more than I can take, but it is so incredibly beautiful I know that it is God. My body and arms become weak. I lose my grip on the ladder and begin to fall through the clouds. As I fall, my eyes fill with tears, because of the beauty I beheld and because of losing sight or union with that beauty.

I woke up saddened, but remembered the emotional onrush brought by the light. I was shuddering with near ecstasy.

If you have ever had an experience where you managed to touch the sense and feeling of the real presence of God and then lost it, you know what this woman means about sadness. Many years later, she still remembers. This dream is a reminder of the great spiritual story of the fall from grace. It is an archetypal dream, meaning it reflects a theme that affects all humans, a theme seen in many times, cultures, and places.

Some folks believe in the literal story of the fall, but that is not how I view it. For me, the story of the fall is a teaching about the development of spiritually oriented, individual consciousness. It is a teaching about our feelings of separation from God as well. Pride and ego-centered individuality, represented by the angel Lucifer in the Western story, act to separate the fallen from God. The result is death, sadness, anger, and fear. Those things lead to extremes of ego-driven, destructive behavior. That is pretty much what we see when we look at the larger world around us and contemplate the way humans act.

An experience of touching the divine is overwhelming and undeniable. It is intense and beyond our usual modes of feeling and thinking. When it passes, we return to the limited awareness of our regular, small-ego self. We are changed, and along with the joy of connection comes the deep sadness of separation. We have touched the fall all over again. It is a reminder to seek anew our spiritual purpose.

This dream is a commentary on the dreamer's spiritual journey. Like most of us, she still has some inner work to do, but the dream provides a glimpse of the divine. That is enough to spur her on.

Dreams from the other side have a common purpose: to inspire us and reconnect us to our intuitive understanding that we are more than just our physical bodies and concerns. The death of a parent, a beloved brother, a favorite grandparent, or another close family member leaves a wound that is slow to heal. We go on, time passes, and the ache recedes until something reminds us of the person and renews the sense of loss. Dreams of those who have gone on can trigger a renewed sense of faith and hope for the dreamer.

He Is Listening

*I want to tell you about a dream I had about my grandmother.
Two months after my grandmother's death, I received a message from her that really has affected my life deeply. My grandmother and I were very close, good friends in life. Not coming from a churchgoing family, often the only talk about spirituality and multisensory experiences came during long conversations with Grandma.*

The setting of the dream was my parents' living room. My mother was sitting in a chair next to Grandma, who was lying on the couch. (Something that she never did in life due to an extreme case of arthritis.) I was standing in the living room and both Mom and I were talking to her. I said, "Do you know how much we will miss you when you're gone?" Grandma said jokingly, "No . . . you won't miss me!"

In protest, my mother claimed, "Oh, yes, we will miss you!" I walked over to Grandma and kissed her on the cheek. At that point, her image faded away to gray. With that kiss, I have never felt such love and peace in all my life. It was a glimpse of a powerful love. All became dark in the dream, and I could hear her voice say slowly and deliberately, with great importance, "Yes, honey . . . he is listening."

I woke up and sat upright in bed, trying to figure out what it all meant and who "he" was. When I suddenly realized it was He, I was shaken.

This dream has effected the course of my life immeasurably. It's not that I didn't believe in God, but I had my moments of doubt.

For this dreamer, the voice of her grandmother reawakened a feeling of love and a connection to spirit. More, it removed doubt in a way that no Sunday sermon could hope to accomplish.

With renewed faith comes personal healing and a sense of acceptance and peace. Those feelings escape us when we are caught in the anger and grief of a loved one's passing. It seems

so unfair, so unjust, especially when someone dies in their prime
or when most of their life seems to lie ahead.

I Love You and Miss You

*My brother T.J. was my best friend. A drunk driver killed him.
I lost my faith in God because my brother was such a good person, and only twenty-two. I could not understand when people
told me, "It was his time." How could it have been his time at
such a young age? I would scream and curse the sky every
night. "Why won't you let me say good-bye? Why can't I see
him one last time?" Then I gave up. I believed I was wasting
my time. No one was listening. I lost my faith in God and was
hurt to think that there was no heaven for my brother.*

*Then, one night, he came to me. Not alive, but in a dream.
I dreamed we were at his funeral, but it was on the beach by
an ocean. I was talking with everyone at the funeral. I happened to glance down the beach, where I saw a light. I started
walking toward the light and noticed it was my brother! A
beautiful light surrounded him. I ran to him, threw my arms
around him, and started crying. He said to me, "Don't worry
about me, I'm safe now. Always know that I love you and I
miss you." I was telling him I loved him and missed him and
I was glad to see him, but I didn't want him to leave. Then he
finished my perfect dream by saying, "The plane ride took forever! But I'm safe now."*

*I woke up with a whole new feeling inside. I now know that
he is safe in heaven, and I pray to God every night now.*

That "whole new feeling" is priceless. I don't think her
brother went to heaven in a plane, but it is a perfect dream symbol for a long journey to the other side.

Many of us lead unhappy lives. We find ourselves in a family
situation where love is in short supply. We do whatever we can to
cope, not always with success. Sometimes, though, there is a

bright light of love in the darkness. Someone cares for us and gives us the acceptance and love we so desperately desire. When that person leaves us, the feeling is devastating. We feel that his or her love has gone as well. But that is not the truth, as this dream tells us.

I Am Always Here

Before this dream, I really didn't have much faith in God or the Bible, or anything like that, although my family is very religious. Especially when my grandmother passed away—she was very, very close to me, closer than my mother and father or anyone else in my family.

There were many questions in my mind. If there was a God, I was very angry with Him for taking away the person I loved most in the world. After a few months passed, I got anxious and scared because the truth had set in, that she had gone from me forever.

One night though, for some reason I prayed. I prayed through tears to see her again. Because of the fear of seeing a ghost (which scares me), the only way I could see her happily would be in a dream, so I prayed for that. That night I had a dream about my grandmother. A lot of it was full of personal things that you probably wouldn't want to hear about, just little things that made me happy being with her. I can tell you we were just having fun laughing and little things like that.

Through everything in my life, she is the only person I felt safe and comfortable with. The dream seemed to last all night. At the end, where we had to say good-bye, I could see she didn't want to leave but she was happy. She told me she was in heaven and it was "her time to go." I started panicking—she told me not to, that she is always here. When I woke up, I thought, "How stupid," but as the morning went on, the dream was as clear as anything. So I thought, "Maybe there is something here." Now, years later, I still remember it clearly. Even though I miss her so much, I feel a little bit better about every-thing. My faith in God is restored and strong.

The next story gives me goose bumps when I read it, because it carries the feeling of the other side so well. It is a true story, just like all the others in this book. I will let you read it before I talk about it.

You Are My Only Friend

I have had a depressed and troubled life. I lost my first husband in a murder/robbery at age twenty-six. Eddie was twenty-seven. I was left alone to raise four children, ages five, three, sixteen months, and three weeks old. After a brief grieving period, I began to have dreams and visions of a little boy calling me. He was standing in the fork of a stream, under a huge tree with small yellow flowers and wild violets covering the ground.

The little boy wore bright orange, like hunters wear. It would sometimes blind me like a bright, white light. This lit-tle boy tried to lure me to him many times. It caused me to have thoughts of dying, and being safe because of this death. For several years, I thought this was an image of my deceased hus-band. Much to my surprise, it wasn't.

After I remarried, I started seeing a hypnotist. During a ses-sion in which I was very emotional, this little boy came to me. He wanted me to play, to go with him to play. The therapist kept telling me, "Tell the little boy no!" I became frightened. The therapist went and got my husband from the lobby and played a holistic healing tape to calm me.

Again, I was put under. Again, the little boy came back and attempted to get me to go with him. I talked to him, with guid-ance from my therapist. He spoke, and I learned that he was not my late husband. The little boy was my older brother. He explained that he died before he could be born. He wanted me to come with him and play. He said I was his only friend, his

87

sister. The therapist made me tell the little boy to leave and not to come back. She made me tell him I could not go with him and that we lived in separate worlds.

After I was brought out from under hypnosis, I told the therapist and my husband that I realized my mother was pregnant with this little boy before she had me, and that she had gone through an abortion. The therapist made me call my parents from her office. I confronted them with my story, and at first they denied it. I then called my grandmother, who confirmed what I knew.

My mother was dating (sleeping with) two different men. She became pregnant. One man was married, and my father was not sure the baby was his. He gave my mother seventy-five dollars and the name of a woman who performed illegal abortions.

This was in the '60s. My mother allowed this woman to place a long, strawlike object in her and blow in a large amount of air, which, in turn, caused a spontaneous miscarriage/abortion. No one had ever told me this story except my unborn sibling during that hypnosis session.

I have not had the dream since I confirmed the truth. When we left the therapist's office that evening, I drew a quick sketch of the stream, tree, and flowers. I showed it to my husband and tucked it away so I would not forget the last place I saw my brother. That recurring dream I had was nothing more than a visit from an angel.

This story is true; my husband can confirm this event. One day, a couple of months after the ordeal with the therapist, I met my husband for lunch. We went to a French restaurant about a mile from his office. We sat on the veranda. After I made my selection from the menu, I looked up and saw a picture of the scene in my dream. There was the tree, the stream, and the flowers. I called my husband's attention to the painting. He immediately asked me if I wanted to leave, but I declined the offer. It was so reassuring. I knew that my brother was safe with Jesus.

Messengers of Love

This story touches me deeply, not least because I can feel the grief this woman faced in her life. It is a story that points out something about dreams that come from the other side: They are not always what they appear to be when we first think about them.

Inspiration means different things to different people. Simple things can inspire us, like the beauty of a summer morning or a friendly word from a neighbor when we are feeling down. We can get our inspiration from sharing our faith with others in community or worship. We can receive a dream that lets us know we are loved and cared for. The message is always the same, in a clear and fundamental way: We are loved, we are not alone, and there is an afterlife where things are all right.

A Smell of Perfume

My grandmother, who was very important in my life and raised me, comes to me about once a year. There is no dialog with her, but I am aware of her being with me. I can smell her perfume and feel her warmth. When I awaken, it takes me a few minutes to realize that it was a dream, because the smells linger. It's such a sweet dream, I never want it to end. I am convinced that she's with me. It is just so real.

This man feels renewed and inspired when his grandmother visits him. Is it only a dream?

No Worries, No Aches and Pains

In 1989, I lost my mom. We were best friends, and this loss was unbearable to me. The burden of cleaning her apartment and getting everything settled was left up to me. I cried a lot and wondered if she was okay. I wondered if she was sick or hot or cold. I worried if she needed me and could not tell me. I could not work. I took several weeks off to take care of things. I was also trying to take care of my three-year-old daughter during all of this. I was a single mom at this time.

After my mom had been gone for about a month, I had the most awesome dream. Sometimes I don't remember my dreams. But this one I remember well, even today. I had this dream that I could feel the same things that my mom was feeling. It was as if I was with her.

It was the most divine feeling I ever had. I had no worries. There was no illness. I had no worries about money; there was no hot or cold, just comfort. No aches or pains. I had a great sense of being complete and feeling wanted and loved. It is a feeling I have never had, nor have I since then. I truly believe it was God's way of letting me know that she was okay.

The dream changed my life. I have always believed in God and heaven, but this made me realize it was all true. I have always been afraid of dying, and I still am, somewhat. This dream let me know that it is a great feeling to be with God. If being in heaven feels like that, then there is nothing to fear. I lost my dad three years after this happened. I handled it a lot better, because I knew the feeling he was going to have.

I love stories like this. They comfort and strengthen those left behind by the death of another. They prepare us for the rest of our journey, including the loss of others along the way. We can face the milestone of a loved one's passing with greater calm and peace, knowing death is neither the end, nor something we must fear. It is the ego, the sense of self intimately tied to physical form, that fears death. We are much more than our ego.

Ego isn't a bad thing, but it is much like a child in the way it perceives things. Fear is lurking around the corner for the ego, and anything that helps soothe the fear and teach us that there is no need to be afraid is valuable. Touching the reality of God and spirit is a sure way to calm the fears.

A dream from the other side can restore our sense of connec-

tion to infinite love. If you have such a dream, let yourself surrender to the feeling and accept it for the gift that it is.

The images of the divine that appear in dreams are consistent with the cultural backgrounds of the dreamers. When people dream of numinous figures, they meet the divine images
that fit their spiritual traditions. "Numinous" means that a figure or dream image carries an inherent quality of the divine,
of God and the sacred mystery. Christians encounter images
familiar in Christian teachings, such as Christ or Mother
Mary. Jews will probably not see Jesus (although it is possible)
but might meet one of the prophets or a biblical image of God.
A Buddhist might see the Buddha himself, although that would
be a lesson in ego and illusion according to Buddhist dream
teaching! Someone from the Muslim tradition might hear the
voice of the Prophet or be advised by an angel. An Aboriginal
tribesman might dream of ancestors or nature beings. Each of
us will meet the image that is suitable for our knowledge and
tradition.

It is also possible to dream of a numinous being who is not
part of your tradition, just to confuse things a little. That makes
sense, though, if you think about it. After all, if some of these
dreams are truly messages from the other side, from another
dimension where spirit takes many forms, we could receive
information in any way that spirit sees fit. It is possible to meet
a master teacher in dreams, who may be from an entirely different culture or tradition than yours. If you have such a dream,
pay attention, and think about what it is that the teacher has
brought to you.

The other side has many dimensions, many doorways to wisdom. We don't have to dream of the dead to get a powerful message that restores and renews our faith in things unseen. Some
of the most powerful images from the other side appear in our
dreams as angels or other spiritual beings. The word "angel"
comes from ancient Hebrew and Greek words that mean "one
who is sent, a messenger."

There are many historical examples of people from all over the world who connected to the divine in dreams. If the dream comes to the right person, world history can change. One example mentioned earlier is the holy book of the Koran, given to the Prophet Muhammad by the angel Gabriel in a series of dreams. No one can deny that Islam has changed the face of the world. The Old Testament, common ground for the three great Western religions of Judaism, Christianity, and Islam, is full of dreams that guide and warn the dreamers, laying out right action and moral or ethical teaching. The prophets, preachers and rulers of the Bible had many visions and dreams. Ezekial, John, and the author of Ecclesiastes are just a few, not to mention Nebuchadnezzar, Moses, Pharaoh, Joseph, King David, and King Solomon. Dreams foreshadowed the virgin birth of the Buddha. Hinduism, too, has a long tradition of dreams and visions providing guidance and spiritual nourishment to those who received them.

It doesn't matter whether we agree with the teachings of these religions or not. What matters is that our dreaming mind is capable of receiving spiritual truth and wisdom. Sometimes the outer mind may filter that wisdom or distort it, sometimes the message is not clear, but the important thing is that it is available to us. It is up to us to put the wisdom to use in our own life.

Most of us will not become the founders of great world religions, which is probably for the best. Even so, many people dream of spiritual beings, of angels speaking to them, of rising to heaven, of walking with Christ or another master teacher, or of great religious figures like the Virgin Mary. I think we get dreams like this when we need reminding that more is going on here than meets our limited, mortal eye. We also receive them, if we are lucky, when we need spiritual guidance.

We are beings of unexplored and unappreciated consciousness, capable of far more than we imagine or experience. In times of trouble, depression, or illness, we may have a dream that brings a feeling for those other dimensions, a dream to remind us of who we really are. Sometimes we get a dream just to let us know that we are pursuing the right path (or the wrong one) in our spiritual journey.

Mother Mary

I am standing on top of a wall outside an enormous stone church. There are thousands of people in the parking lot below, waiting to get into the church. Two women friends are with me.

Then my friends and I are inside the church, at the door to the "inner sanctum," a room lit by tall white candles. A man stops us and lets us know we are not allowed to enter there. He points behind us, to a gigantic room full of chairs where hundreds of people are sitting quietly, waiting their turn, although no one is inside the sanctum. I can't see the faces of the people waiting, because their backs are to me.

The man, an official of the church, begins to recite a long list of regulations that prohibit us from entering the sanctum. I don't feel any particular emotion toward him as he says all this. I feel only a kind of patience, an understanding that he is doing his job as best he knows.

Then I am alone and have gone into the inner sanctum. In the back of the room is a stairway leading up. I climb the stairs, also made of stone. The way is lit by a pure, natural light that gets brighter as I climb higher. The stairs lead to a room at the top of the church—the inner, inner sanctum.

There is a great deal of light coming in through stained glass windows, illuminating Mother Mary sitting in the middle of the room. As we look at each other an absolute light shines through her and grows. It shines into me in such a way as to penetrate all that I am. For a moment I am afraid, but then feel only awe and deep, vibrant love as Mother Mary and I are absorbed into the light.

> *On waking, I feel profoundly refreshed and know that fol-*
> *lowing the rules and doing what I am supposed to do has been*
> *an obstacle to spirit. I know there are hundreds of rules and*
> *hundreds of ways to wait and keep my "place," none of which*
> *lead to this awesome love.*
>
> *I feel a confidence I did not feel before, in life, in the pace of*
> *creativity and in spirit. Whenever I remember walking alone*
> *up the stairs, I am reminded of what is needed from me.*

This is a wonderful dream, a direct spiritual teaching. The symbolism is clear and easy to understand. All those people waiting for permission to enter the inner sanctum are aspects of the dreamer's inner self. They represent the strong part of her that abides by the rules. The man who tells her why she cannot enter the sanctum is more of the same, a symbol of thoughts and perceptions within the dreamer that prevent her from entering the place where she can find what she seeks. What she seeks is true spiritual connection to God. The man in the church is the rule keeper, the part of us that believes in following the rules and does not recognize our right to connect with spirit unless we do it in approved and accepted ways.

This dreamer struggled for years with the restrictions placed upon her by her church. The dream tells her to turn away from the rules and follow the instructions of her heart.

Mother Mary is the embodiment of love, compassion, and nourishment. When the dreamer connects with her it is a transformational experience. More than a dream, it reverberates in her waking life. It gives her a new sense of confidence and purpose, a sense of being on track when she follows her own, intuitive spiritual quest. Truly, a nurturing and sustaining dream from the other side.

Often a dream of spirit serves to steady and reassure the dreamer, even if nothing particularly stressful or challenging is going on in the dreamer's life. A dream can appear when we take on new possibilities or open our life to a different direction.

Walking with Christ

My husband and I are both engineers. Our life is happy, actually pretty close to blissful. At the time of this dream, we had decided to start our own business, which now has great potential.

I was walking along a path in a magnificent meadow: green trees, grasses, flowers, blue sky, utter beauty. I love to walk. I was walking with Christ, just we two. He was explaining things to me, how everything worked. I remember how He pointed things out to me, and how I asked questions. He readily answered and explained. I was so happy to walk with Him, and so satisfied to hear His answers.

Just a little dream of walking with the Master, at a time when things were changing. There's nothing like feeling you are in tune with spirit to take the fear out of new adventures and times of change. For a Christian, dreaming of Christ is a powerful and unforgettable experience.

Glowing Hand

There was one dream I had of Jesus' hand on my shoulder. My room was dark, and his hand had an ethereal glow . . .

This simple dream lifted and reassured the dreamer, and she has never forgotten it. We don't forget dreams of spirit or angels. What does it feel like to have Christ put His hand on your shoulder? Would you forget His touch?

Carry Him Home

When I was about seven, my dad died of a heart attack. When I came home from the funeral, I fell asleep. In my dream, I was at my childhood home and I went behind our barn. My dad was there, and we did everything we used to do when I was very little—for example, we used to play ring-around-the-rosy. Then (in the dream), when the day ended, my dad said he had to go. He walked around the barn and disappeared. Then I saw two angels carrying my dad up into the sky.

The dream made me feel peaceful and happy when I think about my dad. I am not worried or sad that he's dead. I think it was my dad's way of telling me his last good-bye.

This dream is priceless because it healed the grief of a child. This boy was seven when he had the dream. He's older now, but the dream still makes him feel good about his dad.

A Helping Hand

One night shortly after having my second child, I dreamed my deceased father was talking to me. I was telling him that I had a little girl and she was beautiful. My father appeared to me in my dream just as if he were really here.

Later that year, my son (who was about three at the time) woke me to tell me about a dream he had. He dreamed he was in a glowing white tunnel and could not find his way out. Then his angel came and helped him out. That same night, I had a dream I was walking hand in hand with my father and my son in a bright white light. To this day, that dream, which closely resembles my son's, has been very mysterious to me. By the way, my son still dreams of angels, and even comments that he sees them. He is nine now.

How we respond to a dream of a great spiritual being or an angel will depend on our beliefs and spiritual perception. It is a good idea to let go of judgments when listening to someone else talk about a spiritual dream. We might not agree with their beliefs, but that is not the point. The point is that they have received a clear message reaffirming their faith and providing guidance in a way that they can see and understand. This next dream comes from a strong believer in the Christian teachings of heaven and hell.

Actions Guide the Way

A few years ago, when I still lived with my aunt in Florida, I had a dream. It was more like an experience than a dream. In my dream, I had just stepped outside my door when I noticed there was a glowing object down the street that seemed to stop at every house. It stopped only to look and then it would continue on, going from house to house. I began walking away when suddenly this figure was upon me. It looked very unclear at first, shining bright with magnificence. Then a face became definite; I'm not sure if it was male or female. The face had a perfect appearance, with wavy blond hair and blue eyes. There was some sense of familiarity about this angel; I believe it may have been my guardian angel.

We exchanged few words. My only question for the angel was about my entrance into heaven. My uncle was a sore point with me at the time. The angel looked down at me and, with the most beautiful voice one could hear, told me my actions would guide my way. The angel told me that, for the most part, I was on the right path, but there were areas in my life that needed to change in order for me to make it. For my uncle, the news wasn't quite as refreshing. The angel said that my uncle had failed by his actions. His addictions would lead him to the gates of hell.

This dream helped me realize that the road I was on was not the path God had chosen for me, and that I needed to change my ways to serve Him better. I only wish I would have this dream again, so I could remember more and ask questions about things that just aren't clear to me. The dream was frightening in a sense, but I am so happy to have experienced it. I pray we could all experience just a taste of God's glory so that we all would know how wonderful our Father is.

I don't think her uncle will go to hell, I think there is only love on the other side. That part of her dream is a reflection of her beliefs and a comment on the difficult relationship with her uncle and her unhappiness about it. Sometimes our personal issues and ideas about life get mixed up with the message that is coming through. It is one of those things that makes it hard to discern what is a true dream of return and what is not.

The next dream mirrors our desire to find divine love, to experience that love and know that we are not alone. In an earlier part of the dream (not given here), the dreamer is searching for something he loves and has lost. He is distraught, worried, fearful, and very upset. He comes to a place where he sees a figure and asks him if he knows where to find what he is looking for.

You've Found It

Looking into my eyes, with what seemed like the most divine light that I have ever seen, he says, "Here I am." He pulls off his "covering" of humanness, and all I can see is light, all I can feel is his words entering my head as he tells me my search is over. He tells me I have found love, that it has always been with me. I just refused to see it.

Music filled the place where we were, and we started to dance. I felt like an angel. I was light and full of love and it was a few minutes before I realized I was dreaming, and I woke up. All events were "shown" to me. Awakening from this dream, I felt as if God Himself had given me a direct message.

I cried for a good long time, real tears, upon awakening. The impact of the dream was such that I wrote it down. The words I kept repeating on the page were "love," "love," and "love." It may sound corny or clichéd, but the inspiration from the dream lingers on, and I am a firm believer that love is all there is. It is always with us, and we must remember to show it, appreciate it, find it, give it, and, sometimes, be prepared to lose it.

I cannot think of a more direct or more profound spiritual teaching than the injunction to show love, appreciate it, and give it. It is also true that we often forget and lose the sense of it. Perhaps the sense of needing and losing love spurs us to greater spiritual efforts—I don't know. I do know that love is the fundamental message of all true spiritual teaching, from whatever tradition or culture.

A very large number of people are seeking spiritual understanding and guidance these days. Several books have become huge best-sellers because they resonate with a need people have to understand what we are doing here and what it is all about. The spiritual quest is alive and well.

Everything Is a Part of God

I had just put down a book I was reading called Conversations with God. *Every night I was feeling confused about what I should believe, regarding life on earth. That night my eyes opened to new possibilities. Inside I felt I was ready to know the truth about God and about who "we" are.*

I finally fell asleep. The next thing I knew I was on the floor in a dream, talking and laughing with a beautiful golden light. I had no doubt in my mind that I was indeed having my own conversation with God. I told this beautiful spirit that I could not believe how much fun it was. It laughed and asked me where I thought fun came from. It then told me that it was time for me to wake up. I replied, "But I don't want to go, I'm having so much fun and I don't want to leave you." God said "You can't leave me, and I can't and won't leave you, I am always with you, in all ways. So go now, and have fun today." I said, "Okay, I love you," and God said, "I love you, too."

From that moment on I knew who we were and why we are here. Most of all, I learned that God, our creator and our friend, expects nothing from us. Everything we do and everything we are is a part of God already.

"Everything we do and everything we are is a part of God already." That fundamental spiritual teaching crosses all barriers of time and culture. It is more than just an idea. Recognizing this truth is a major step for the spiritual seeker. It might take a lifetime or so to integrate what this statement means, but recognition of the truth of it is fundamental to spiritual growth. We are not separate from God. We are not alone. We are loved.

People often share dreams with me that address personal issues in their lives, dreams using religious symbolism that fits with the dreamer's beliefs about God and spirit. I have not included many of those in this book, although they often feature angels or other spiritual figures. These kinds of dreams fall into what I term the psychological category and are not truly dreams from the other side. They are powerful for the dreamers, though. Here is an example of what I mean.

To a Safe Place

Last night I had a dream that there was a war, there was shelling and bombing. Angels took me to a safe place.

This is a psychological dream, where angels represent something that can guide her away from a conflict taking place in her own unconscious mind, symbolized by the war in the dream. The good news is that she is rescued, so we can predict things will work out for her and that she will discover the solution to her conflict.

In general, a true dream from the other side will have a much different quality to it than the psychological kind. One thing consistent to dreams that cross the barrier is a feeling of great love. There may well be guidance given, but there is never condemnation or judgment of the dreamer.

If we are wrestling with feelings of inadequacy or judging ourselves harshly, we might get a dream where our "sins" are brought to our attention and judgment is threatened. That is especially likely if we are fervent believers. Many religious teachings feature judgment and the threat of terrible punishment. If you get a dream like that, consider it as a message from your inner self, not from the other side. All I can say is that experience tells me the real thing comes wrapped in clouds of love and acceptance.

Chapter 4

•—•—••—••—•—•—••—••—•—•—••—•—•—•—••—••—•—••—•—••—•—••—•—••—•—••—•—••—•—•

Someone to Watch over Me

•—•—••—••—••—•—••—•—••—•—••—••—•—••—••—•—•—••—••—•—••—••—•—••—•—••—•—••—•—••—•

Follow my lead, oh how I need, someone to watch over me.
—IRA GERSHWIN

W E ALL WANT AND NEED someone to watch over us, to guide us and care for us along the way. Some of the most wonderful dreams are ones where a beloved person returns and lets us know someone is looking out for us, paying attention and keeping watch. It comforts us to feel the presence of a loved one no longer in physical form. Sometimes the message has real implications in the real world for the dreamer, beyond the peaceful joy of reunion.

One thing I noticed gathering material for this book is how often a loving grandparent returns in a dream. If we are lucky enough to have the kind of extended family that includes kind

103

grandparents, we are likely to form a special relationship with them very different from the one we have with our parents. It is easy to relate to caring grandparents when we are children. After all, they indulge us, enjoy the best moments, and then send us back home! Grandparents tend to be more forgiving and less dictatorial, at least in families where love is the foundation of relationship.

These next two dreams are from the same dreamer. The first dream is a good example of a "watch over me" kind of dream. It brought a wonderful sense of peace and calm to the dreamer. The second dream is quite special, as you will see.

Don't Worry, I'm Very happy

I was very close to my grandmother and for the five or six years before she died, I visited with her at least twice a week and called her on the phone several times a week. I really thought of her as one of my close friends, and we talked about so many things. She died after a relatively short bout with lung cancer. The last few months my family would take turns on "death watch"—one day and night a week, when each of the seven of us would stay with her, keep my grandfather fed and the house cleaned, and administer her medications.

About nine months after she died, I had this dream. I dreamt I was at a party at my parent's house. There were many people there. Granny was there, too, having a wonderful time. In fact, everyone was having a wonderful time. My parents used to have parties like this for any occasion—football games, birthdays, July Fourth—any excuse to get together, play in their band, and enjoy other people. Due to Granny's illness and the death of her son about three years before, we had not had one of these parties in a long time.

At this particular dream party, everyone was really having a great time. Granny and I were having a conversation, and then she left to go socialize with some of the other guests. I con-

tinued to enjoy the party, and then Granny came back into the room, but she was about ten years younger. We talked for awhile and she left again. This coming and going went on, and each time she left, she came back about ten years younger. Finally, she came in and she was my age. We sat and talked for a long time, and she eventually stood up, took my hand, and said, "Honey, this is the last time you're going to see me for awhile. But don't worry, I'm very happy and I'll be watching over you." She then beamed a smile at me, turned, and quietly walked out the door. I woke up with the most wonderful and peaceful feeling.

That dream would be more than enough to make anyone feel good about a real, ongoing connection after death. The next dream deepens the connection and takes it to another level.

The Next One Will Be Yours to Take Care Of

I was seven weeks pregnant with my second pregnancy. I miscarried my first pregnancy at twelve weeks and was really worried, but still hopeful, about this pregnancy. In my dream, I was standing in a cloudy, bright haze. Granny emerged from the haze and had two little girls with her. One child was about one year old, and the other was not much more than a doll in my Granny's hands. Granny said, "I just thought you might like to meet your daughters."

I realized right then that my first baby was really in heaven with my Granny, and that I would lose this pregnancy also. I'm sure Granny saw the look on my face, because then she said, "The next one will be yours to take care of." When I woke up, I had this beautiful peaceful feeling, even though I knew I had started the process of miscarrying. My beautiful, healthy son Gabriel was born a year later. When I awoke from this dream, I felt such a feeling of calm and peace. I knew Granny and my babies were happy and whole in the next world.

Isn't that a wonderful story? There is not any way to explain a dream like that using conventional theories, at least not any way that would satisfy me. Because of that dream, the dreamer was able to accept her second miscarriage, knowing there would be another child. The dream forewarned her of the second loss and showed her those two children safe with her grandmother in the afterlife. I'd say Granny was doing a pretty good job of looking out for her granddaughter.

It seems the other side may not be so far away after all. The barrier that separates this world from the next is a lot closer and a lot thinner than we think.

Trouble in the Family

My uncle came to me in a dream when I was living in Santa Fe, New Mexico. He told me there was going to be "trouble in my family" and I should come home (back to Seattle). Just like a movie, I saw things done by family members concerning a large amount of money I was going to inherit. My dreams have guided me continually as to what to do and the situation is going to be resolved justly and with love. It was all accomplished because I had such guidance from the other side in dreams.

Love knows no veil, no divide between the living and the dead. When there is need for reassurance and support, love finds a way to cross the gap between the two realities. The support and love of her uncle helped her keep an even keel and deal lovingly with the divisive issue of her inheritance while protecting her interests.

Don't Worry, They'll Be Just Fine

Five years ago, I entered the hospital thirty-four weeks into my pregnancy with preeclampsia, while carrying my twins. My OB decided my condition was deteriorating and planned an induction.

Early that morning (around 5:00 A.M.) I woke up excited but decided to try to fall asleep again since my induction was not planned for at least two more hours. At some point shortly thereafter, I dreamed about my grandmother and grandfather. My grandmother was carrying both my children in her arms. She brought them to me and told me they were going to be just fine and not to worry. My grandfather did not speak, although that was not unusual for him. He was a quiet person.

At 12:19 P.M. and 12:25 P.M. my babies were born. My daughter was perfectly healthy, but my son was blue and needed oxygen. Forty-five minutes after his birth, I was told that if he lived through the night, he had a fifty-fifty chance of survival. Throughout the days following the birth, I was concerned about my son but calm. I am convinced that my grandmother came to me to let me know that she was watching over them and that my son was meant to live. Today he is a happy, healthy five-year-old who has had no further complications of any kind.

Like the woman earlier who dreamed that the "next one will be yours to keep," this woman was able to relax and let go of much fear and worry about her baby. She had reassurance from the other side that all would be well.

One of the things we miss when we lose someone we love is the chance to share important things in our lives with them. We enjoy sharing good things with our loved ones, and we want them to feel our happiness. After they pass over, we have just our thoughts and memories, and perhaps some things we wish we had said before it was too late. Even after years have passed, we may wonder what someone we loved might think of the happenings in our lives. We may wish they could see and approve of how things are going with us. They do.

Dreams from the Other Side

Do You Think I Would Miss Your Wedding?

I had this dream in 1963, just before my marriage. I was getting married to someone my father had disapproved of before his death. He died when I was twelve. I was concerned about what he would think of me and my choice for a husband, especially since my mother and my future husband's father were less than thrilled about the marriage.

Anyway, I don't remember where I was or what I was doing but suddenly my father was there in my dream and it became as real as if he were right next to me. He was on a horse (he loved to ride) and he was in his favorite kind of clothes (jeans and a white Western shirt with a bolo string tie). He had on his cowboy boots. The only thing missing was his black Stetson. Instead, he wore one of those "booney" or Australian-style hats that are pinned up on one side. (He was in the South Pacific during World War II, but I'm not sure if the hat is significant.) I told him how glad I was to see him and asked him why he had come to see me, or something to that effect. He said, "Do you think I would miss your wedding?"

I woke up with the most wonderful feeling that my dad loved me and didn't disapprove of my then future husband. It remains one of the most vivid and easily remembered dreams I have ever had.

I doubt anything else could resolve her concerns like that dream. She couldn't very well ask her father for his blessing in real life, could she? Yet he found a way to let her know that all was well.

During a stressful or worrisome time, we may get a dream of return about someone we loved, come to reassure us that all will be well. Financial loss, job worries, health problems—all of the stressful things of life may trigger a visitation. It is a wonderful gift to connect with the feeling that all will be well, after all. Sometimes calm support is the best medicine.

At the Hospital

I dreamed of my deceased father. In January, my granddaughter was having her tonsils removed and the next day I was having a lump removed from my breast. Dad was at the hospital, standing at a hospital bed with the family. He left the group and turned to look at me. I felt very calm about both surgeries. We both came out okay.

Everyone I know gets concerned when faced with some surgical procedure. Even if it is a relatively minor thing, we all know that surgery exposes us to many risks and possible complications, including death or a bad prognosis. Our state of mind is critical to how we handle the stress and the operation itself. In my private practice, I often use hypnosis to help people prepare for surgery. The emphasis is on relaxation, release of fear, and the miraculous powers of mind, body, and spirit for healing. Once the mind gets the message that everything will be okay, we relax and get the best possible benefit from the surgery. Getting a dream like the one above is worth several sessions in a hypnotherapist's office!

Put Your Mind at Peace

My name is Mary Lee and I will be fifty this year. After my marriage of twenty-five years ended, and after a couple of "being used" relationships, I wondered if I would ever meet someone who would love me through this life and, if possible, into the next.

I wasn't looking, wasn't interested in getting my heart broken. Then, one night I met Frank, one year older than me. We hit it off instantly and have been together for about year.

Recently, I was having some concerns about our relationship, if it was to continue and the depth of his commitment. Emotionally, I had been on edge for several weeks, but keeping my concerns inside.

One night I had a dream of a very lovely older woman. Her hair was radiant white and she was wearing a white gown. There seemed to be a very gentle breeze around her. Although I had only seen pictures of her as a young, dark-haired woman, I knew right away that she was Frank's mother. There was such a feeling of peace with her. She touched my shoulder and said, "Put your mind at peace, he loves you very much." I started to speak about my concerns for our relationship. She stopped me before I got two words out and said, "He loves you very much, put your mind at peace."

With that, she smiled and went away. I was overcome with joy and such calm it can't be put into words. When I awoke early in the morning, I woke Frank and told him that his mother had come to me. I described what she looked like, and what she said, and related how she made me feel.

He asked me how I knew she had snow white hair and had been buried in a white dress. I had no way of knowing, because she died two years before Frank and I met. He asked me how I knew that she often touched the shoulder of the loved one she was speaking with. I had no way of knowing her mannerisms because I had never met her or heard about her life habits.

All I know is the feeling of peace that she conveyed to me with her presence and her words and touch. What she told me has helped me through some difficult times. Frank wondered why she came to me and has never appeared to him. I don't know the answer to that question. I only know how thankful I am for her words of encouragement.

Uncertainty in relationship is one of the most stressful experiences we will ever have. It is a true blessing to get past it in spite of fears all might not go well. Whatever the problems in her relationship with Frank, the reassurance brought by the dream comforted Mary Lee in a way nothing else could. How did Mary Lee know those intimate details about Frank's mother? The only explanation that makes sense is that Mother paid a visit in the dream. How else would you explain it?

You Go on from Here

When I was sixteen years old, I had a dream that I was walking in a forest between my father's twin brothers. One passed away a few years before I was born, and the other when I was eighteen months old. One was a talented cartoonist and the other was good at writing. In the dream, we reached a small wooden bridge over a small creek. When we reached the middle of the little bridge, they told me they could not go any farther, and I would have to go on by myself.

From the age of four to eighteen, I wanted to be an artist. I spent all my spare time drawing and painting (until the age of fifteen, when I also began writing poetry). I majored in art, won several awards from grammar school through high school, but did not really have the talent to be a true artist. For several years after that dream, I felt that I was not me but a combination of these two men, whom I loved although I never knew them, and who lost their lives so early. I do have a memory of one of them that I told my mother and sister when I was older. They remembered it as well, and I was shocked to realize that I was only eighteen months old at the time.

We are never alone. There is someone watching over us, paying attention to us in a caring and compassionate way, without judgment or hidden agenda. This woman has had unpleasant times in her life, but the dream of her father's brothers helped her through them. The bridge in the dream is symbolic of the barrier between the dead and the living, and the message is consistent with the "rules" of contact. The dead can guide, warn, and support, but they cannot live our life for us or tell us exactly what to do in any situation. We have free will and our own path to follow, our own decisions to make, and our own consequences of those decisions. It is not lawful for those on the other side to tell us what to do. We have to figure it out for ourselves.

Almost all the dreams in these pages inspired and lifted the dreamer. That does not mean a dream of the dead will not be disturbing, though. Fear can prevent following through on the message, even when a strong feeling of love is present in the dream. I hope if you have one of these dreams, you will not be afraid to follow through. This next story is from a young woman who lives in England. She has not followed up on her dream, because it frightened her. Until she does, we will never know why the dream came to her.

Contact My Friend

I am eighteen years old. About eighteen months ago, I had a dream that disturbed me greatly.

At about this time I felt very much alone and in a lot of emotional pain. My mother was very sick in hospital. I had just been told I had a genetic disorder that would stop me from having children. I was finding life impossible to cope with and had nobody to turn to. My parents are divorced, and the only other member of my family I could talk to was my nan, who was on holiday.

In the dream, I am alone in the house where I live. I am sad and sitting on my bed when I hear the phone ringing downstairs in the hallway.

I feel scared and apprehensive about picking up the phone, but the ringing is so loud I have to. When I answer, I hear a man's voice. It is deep and kind, and I know that it is my grandfather. He passed away when my mum was young. I never had a chance to meet him. He was brief on the phone and gave me a message to pass on.

He asked me to contact a man named "Nobby" (a nickname) who lived in Faversham where he had lived. He told me the house number and that I should make it clear that I was his granddaughter. When I awoke, I wrote this down for my nan and called to tell her. It turns out that her husband (my dead grandfather) had a close friend when he was growing up whose name was Robert, but his nickname was Nobby.

I have not contacted this man and I have not had another dream like this, but I believe there is an afterlife and that I was meant to deliver that message. If this is published, I prefer to remain anonymous. I hope this has helped.

This dream arrived by way of my Web site, without a return address, so I have no way of contacting this dreamer or knowing where she lives. If I could correspond with her, I would encourage her to go ahead and attempt making the connection with Nobby. There must be a reason why her grandfather contacted her during a particularly bad time in her life. Perhaps she will read this book and decide to make the effort—I hope so.

PSYCHIC AND PROPHETIC DREAMS

An American woman I know well was traveling in England some time ago and had this next dream. Louise is somewhat psychic and if she needed any proof of her abilities, this dream ought to be enough! There are many dreams in this book, but this is one of the strangest as far as I am concerned.

I Was an Older Man

I looked at my face in a bathroom mirror and noticed that I was an older man. I studied my features for a moment, and then I got on a boat. A short time later, the boat exploded.

I found myself without a body, just a disembodied consciousness. Then, I realized I was dead. . . . I woke up with a start. The dream troubled me and I told it to my husband at the time.

Later, I saw a photo on the front page of a newspaper and immediately recognized the face in my dream. It was Lord Mountbatten, assassinated by a terrorist bomb on his boat. I had been asleep and dreaming at the exact moment of his death. Somehow, I experienced it with him.

I have no idea why Louise would dream of Mountbatten, nor does she. As an American, she had no reason to be familiar with this famous man, so well known in England. She did not even know who he was, much less what he looked like. Yet, she seems to have been with him in her dreaming consciousness for a short time before and at his death. That dream would trouble me also.

Dreaming of someone's death before it occurs is much more common than dreaming of death as it occurs. The people I know who have these kinds of dreams are not happy about it. They would much rather not have the gift. I don't think I would want it either, but we do not have that choice. We either have the ability or we do not.

I Still Dream of These Things

When I was fourteen years old, I dreamed of my mother in a coffin and an angel who came to visit me. A year later, my mother passed away of cancer. I also dream of others before they pass away. I am now forty and still dream of these things.

Sometimes I dream of people who have passed, and they are not just family members but friends. It bothers me, because I do not know what they are trying to tell me.

These folks are appearing in her dreams because she has psychic ability and somehow tunes in to their impending deaths. The people in her dreams may not be telling her anything in a direct sense. What they are telling her by implication is that their time of transition is approaching. Perhaps she could use that knowledge to help them in some way, or their loved ones. Unfortunately, anyone who comes knocking with a prediction of death will not be welcome. That is a problem with unpleasant prophecy.

Prophecy is a kind of dream from the other side, almost never welcome. Usually it foretells something we do not want to know about. Although we can get dreams prophesying a good result, most prophetic dreams deal with things more traumatic and disturbing.

It is easy to understand why a dream from the other side might be unwanted. After all, we are talking about the dead, about people (even those we love) who have left behind physical form and crossed the veil. We call it "the veil" with good reason. We cannot see beyond it, we fear it, we know that one day we, too, will be confronted with the reality of the end of life. Nevertheless, isn't it comforting to think there really is an afterlife and that we will find a home in it?

Death frightens us because it is a gateway to the unknown. We are uncomfortable with what we don't know, and death is the biggest mystery of all. Part of the problem stems from world religious teachings that confuse the issue of life after death with terrible predictions of hellish eternities and awful punishments waiting for us beyond death's door. All of us have made mistakes, all of us are imperfect, and all of us have been taught, one way or another, that we should feel guilty about something. We fear the possibility of divine judgment. Yet one of the true and golden threads of all genuine spiritual wisdom is the theme of unconditional, nonjudgmental love.

Each of us has to come to our own conclusion about the existence and nature of the afterlife. What we will decide is shaped by many cultural, traditional, and personal factors. Those factors will determine if we believe in an afterlife and if we fear judgment at death.

What I notice is that most dreams from the other side present us with images of love, comfort, and the removal of the burdens and sorrows we bear during life. They do not present us with dire threats and warnings of terrible judgment if we do not mend our ways. Even the dream given earlier, where an angel seems to comment on the misdeeds of the dreamer's uncle, can be understood within the context of the dreamer's beliefs and the kind of religious symbolism familiar to her. The dream inspired her to rethink her relationship with God, which was the point.

DREAM GUIDANCE FOR OTHERS

Sometimes a dream comes to someone not directly related to the deceased, with a message for someone who is. Some years ago, I knew a man (I will call him Ethan) who became seriously ill with liver disease. He received a transplant at the last possible moment, continued to live for a few more years, and died. Left behind were his wife, Yvon, and young daughter, Adria.

I knew Ethan and his family from their participation in many spiritual, metaphysical, and community events. Ethan's daughter, Adria, was the joy of his life. Ethan was a metaphysical writer, could see auras, and was occasionally quite psychic. Dreams and the exploration of life's spiritual mysteries fascinated him. During his illness and nearing the time of his death, he made it clear that he would try to communicate from the other side with his family.

Years passed. After some time, Yvon met someone and eventually remarried. The marriage was soon compromised by the actions of her charismatic and psychologically immature husband. At times charming and creative, he also carried a hidden dark side that caused tremendous problems for Yvon and Adria. Chronically unable to tell the truth, he created a tangled web of deceit, financial ruin, police involvement, and an unhappy, destructive home life.

These years had a very strong, negative effect on Adria. Yvon's new husband was unable to understand or integrate Adria's confusion as she hit adolescence. He responded with anger and attempts to assert rigid control. Adria is intelligent, psychic, and sensitive, which only made things more difficult. Trouble was brewing. Then, a close friend of Yvon's had the following dream.

There is a Crisis Brewing

In the dream, I go to Yvon's house to visit. She shows me some work she has been doing—the house is larger, the life force more vibrant.

Yvon is busy preparing for an event. We walk outside, into a parklike setting. As I walk down a pathway, I see a man approaching me. He is unusually dressed. He has on rust-colored, velvetlike bell-bottom pants and a matching top. He wears a symbol on a chain and a funky 1970s-style velvet hat with a rim on it, a Mamas and Papas kind of hat. His eyes are dark brown, intense. His skin is clear and he is slim and in good shape. It is Ethan!

I say, "Ethan, is that you?" He says, "Yes, come and walk with me, I want to talk with you about Yvon and Adria."

I begin to walk with him and we end up sitting on a grassy knoll beneath the walkway, near a stream. I am fascinated that I can see Ethan. I tell him how exciting it is that I can actually see him. I blink several times and I still see him. I remark how I have seen those on the other side in dreams and several vague apparitions, but never an ongoing physical viewing and presence like this. He smiles and is amused as I keep blinking to see if he will still be there. I say, "If you are so real to my eyes, will you be real to my touch, too?" He reaches over and gives me a hug. I accept the fact that I am really speaking to and seeing Ethan.

As we speak, he tells me of his love for Adria. He says that he always brushes her cheek gently with a father's loving kiss from the other side. He tells me to tell Yvon that he is watching over Adria and her development. Then he says that he has a message that he needs me to deliver to Yvon. I ask him what the message is.

He leans over and touches me on the third eye, and dream symbols appear before me. I see some kind of intrigue, I see old men with their heads wrapped and long gray beards and long robes. These elders seem to have something to do with religion and morals. They are unhappy and there is danger involved with their presence. I feel intimidated by them and feel they are angry about something. I hear them speak of spring of this year. Then I hear Ethan's voice again.

"Tell Yvon there is a crisis brewing, but that I will be working from this side to dissipate the energy and lighten the karmic effects of this lesson. The lesson can be transmuted through wisdom, intelligence, and knowledge." At this moment, I felt that Ethan's message would serve to alter or transcend some impending event in Yvon and Adria's life.

I wake up with the telephone ringing, still half asleep and in the dream. I know it is Yvon on the phone, so I stumble downstairs, look at the answering machine, see that it was her, and call her back. She knew I was sleeping and had not expected to hear from me right away. I tell her the dream.

Remember, the dead speak to us in the symbolic language of dreams, as well as giving us direct messages of love or warning. This dream is a good example of how the two combine to give a full picture. Like many dreams that refer to future events, we can understand this one best in hindsight, since the nature of the impending threat or problem is not obviously stated. At the time of the dream, it was impossible to determine the nature of the coming crisis.

All we know from the dream is that something is going to happen, possibly in the spring, and that Ethan will be "working from this side" to soften the effects. We also know that Ethan wants Yvon to be aware that trouble is on the way. The only thing Yvon could do was try to stay aware of any developing events that might fit the definition of "a crisis brewing." That is not much help when you are raising a troubled teenager who has become sexually aware, in an environment of control, mistrust, and suspicion. In that situation, you could say that every day had the potential for crisis!

Adria, meanwhile, was an outcast at her school. In every school there are kids who fit in and kids who do not. Adria was one of the ones who did not. Adults tend to categorize school students by things like athletic and scholastic success, participation in officially approved events, and by social groupings. Adria's social group was into the Goth look, wearing black, piercing body parts, and in general being as rebellious and different as possible from what school authorities thought was correct and appropriate. In Colorado, since the Columbine school shootings, there is a very paranoid and suspicious atmosphere in schools on the part of administrators and teachers. Adria fell into one of the groupings that draws extra attention and concern.

What the dream foreshadowed was a series of incidents at school that could have led to a lot of trouble for Adria. The first incident took place in early spring, when she went to school in a dress and cape. That was all right, until she took the cape off in the cafeteria at lunchtime and revealed that her dress was slit up to her waist and that she was not wearing underwear! This caused an explosion of attention (which certainly fulfilled one of Adria's needs). She was sent home in gym shorts and a T-shirt; her clothes were confiscated and dire warnings of expulsion and worse filled the air.

The second incident, one that could have triggered the full paranoia of Columbine's aftermath, took place because of a fight that Adria had with one of her Goth boyfriends. In a dramatic gesture reminiscent of a nineteenth-century romantic, he came to school the next day and handed her a vial of his blood. Students who witnessed the exchange panicked and ran to the teachers. Adria placed the vial in her locker, not knowing what else she should do with it.

Authorities soon arrived on the scene, searched her locker, and found the blood. They also found a mobile of mutilated Barbie dolls, created with her mother's knowledge as a kind of therapeutic outlet for some of Adria's darker thoughts of self-mutilation and punishment.

Her friend was expelled. That could have been Adria's fate as well, but instead she received only a mild warning. Yvon thinks, as do I, that this was because Ethan was doing his work from the other side to lessen the consequences and impact of the events.

It is hard to explain the atmosphere of fear and concern that seems to permeate public schools in the wake of Columbine. Often we hear stories of students expelled for having a nail clipper or a couple of Tylenols, or for making a comment like, "I could have killed him!" For a kid marked down as a troublemaker, as Adria was, expulsion for a year would have been a real possibility, although she was an unwilling participant in the drama of the blood. The Barbie dolls alone would have been enough to get her in big trouble.

The dream was accurate about crisis in the spring. In hindsight, the dream figures of the elders are symbolic of the school authorities. By showing figures of authoritative, angry, and judgmental elders, Ethan was showing her one essential facet of the crisis that would happen.

During the same period, Adria became sexually active. That alone would be enough to explain the dream and Ethan's intervention. In the aftermath of these events, Adria entered therapy. She is doing well, her marks are up to honor roll standards, and she is working through the self-destructive impulses that brought her close to the edge. She has become a peer counselor, turning her rebellion against convention and authority into a positive resource for others.

Chapter 5

•—••—••—••—••—••—••—••—••—••—••—••—••—••—••—••—••—••—•

At the Banks
of the River

•—••—••—••—••—••—••—••—••—••—••—••—••—••—••—••—••—••—•

I looked over Jordan and what did I see, coming for to carry me home?
A band of angels, coming after me, coming for to carry me home.
  —FROM THE OLD SPIRITUAL, "SWING LOW, SWEET CHARIOT"

S TORIES, TEACHINGS, AND SACRED MYTHS prepare us for the
passage through death. Each culture has unique images
and symbols for the final separation from physical life. One
image recurring in many cultures is a broad river. Someone
waits at the shore to guide us further or to take us across.

In Greek mythology, the underworld is called Hades. Hades
has often substituted for hell in the West. When you died in
ancient Greece, you came to the near shore of the River Styx.
The Greeks did not think of the journey to the underworld as a
pleasant one. Picture yourself standing in a gray twilight, sur-

rounded by terrified, confused souls. Before you flows a great river, dark, broad, and silent, that marks one of the boundaries of the underworld. A terrible three-headed dog guards the way, sniffing out any living soul that might try to sneak in. His master is Charon, fearful and silent ferryman of souls.

Charon took only those who could pay his fare across the black waters. The old custom of placing coins on a dead person's eyes or in the mouth of the corpse comes from these times. The coins paid the ferryman's toll. If you could not pay, you were left to wander aimlessly for eternity on the barren, twilit shore of the river. That is not a very pleasant thought about the afterlife!

The classical Greek underworld seems to have been mostly a dark and gloomy place. Sometimes when you crossed the Styx, you drank from the river of forgetfulness. Then you no longer remembered anything of your previous life, considered a blessing for some. If your life as an ancient Greek had been a good and fruitful one, you eventually came to the Elysian fields, called the abode of the blessed, the best that the underworld had to offer. This was where the Greek heroes came at death. Elysium was located in the West, at the end of the world. In later centuries, Elysium was transformed into the blessed Isle of Avalon, famous from the Arthurian legends.

The Egyptians also saw the soul taking a boat journey, but it was far more elaborate than the later Greek version and fraught with perils overcome by spiritual knowledge and a pure heart. The newly dead endured many hazardous adventures, fighting snakes and crocodiles, winning through only with the help of the gods. Eventually one emerged into the light, where existence resumed in much the same fashion as it had been lived during life.

Dreams will signal when it is time for our soul to come to the banks of the river.

Most dreams featuring symbols of death are not actually about the physical end of life. Seeing yourself lying in a coffin in a dream does not mean you are booked for a journey to the great beyond. It is hard for most of us to think about our own death or the deaths of those we love, yet a dream that truly foretells the passing can be a gift and a blessing. It challenges us to master our fears and feelings of loss and to accept the inevitable. It gives us a chance to prepare.

I remember seeing a wonderful television segment some years ago that featured one of these dreams. I do not remember the name of the show—it was about the mystery of death and some of the spiritual and unexplained phenomena that can happen in life. In the show, the story was told of a dying woman in her hospital bed. The camera zoomed in on the dying patient. A glowing candle sat on the windowsill of her room. She fell asleep and dreamed of the candle. In her dream, she saw the flame slowly dying out until it disappeared. For a moment there was blackness—then the candle reappeared, burning on the *other* side of the window, outside her room. She woke and told the dream. Soon after, she died peacefully.

Can you feel the beautiful symbolism of the images? This is a dream that foretells death, and promises rebirth and renewal on the other side. The dream candle represents her life force, flickering to an end. The extinction of the candle flame signals the end of her life. The moment of darkness symbolizes the transition through death's gateway. The window is a symbol of the barrier between this life and the next. When the candle reappears on the other side of the window, burning anew, it is a reassuring symbol of the certainty there is nothing to fear. The essence of who we are continues. The dream was a story for her own comfort and passing, a way to let her know she could relax and let go.

That particular dream came to that particular woman, but it is a sign of comfort for all of us. We are renewed on the other side. Death is not the end, and we need not fear what comes after.

Dreams can come to us about our own death, or the death of another. A very good friend of mine has had psychic dreams foreshadowing the death of friends and family members for years. She is an intelligent and educated person, a practicing psychologist. She never liked having these dreams. Most people who have a consistent history of dreaming about unpleasant things that come true wish they did not have the gift, which seems more like a curse than a boon.

Miriam comes from an Orthodox Jewish background, her family was observant of prayer and tradition. She is a successful author and has written a book about death and dying. Some years ago, she had a dream that repeated three times. In the dream, family members who had already passed on were reciting the prayers to the dead for Miriam's aunt, at the time still alive. Miriam took this to mean she should help this aunt prepare for death.

Miriam was not especially close to her aunt, and in fact had been out of touch with her, but she took the time to reconnect. Part of Miriam's life involves a dedicated and profound spiritual seeking and practice. She is committed to service. She spent hours at her aunt's bedside almost every day, talking with her aunt, helping her focus on her beliefs and her thoughts about the afterlife. Not long after, the aunt died.

When a dream repeats itself exactly, and when that dream focuses on an image of death of someone, it is a good idea to consider it seriously. Sometimes this kind of dream is about transition or psychological change within the dreamer, symbolized by the dead person in the dream, but is not referring to physical death. Miriam, though, with her psychic experiences and her broad knowledge of the process of death and dying, chose to see the dream as foreshadowing death and acted according to the dictates of her heart. She was right.

Miriam had another dream of death, this time about one of her sons, but death was averted. In the dream, she saw her son in a terrible car accident. Three skulls appeared in the dream, which she interpreted as symbolic markers of his death. With her history of death dreams coming true, Miriam feared for his life. Unable to control events in any direct way that might avoid the accident, she turned to prayer. She spent an entire day in intense prayer, hoping all would be well.

Not long after, her son was involved in a serious car accident, just as in the dream, but he walked away from the wreck. I saw the car after the event. It was a miracle that her son survived. In this case, the dream warned of death approaching but prayer changed the outcome.

I remember one woman, whom I will call Jeanine, who taught me a very powerful lesson about dreaming and life's endings. She was around thirty years old, a mother of young children, recently remarried and in a loving relationship. She also had terminal cancer. She was participating in a two-week residential retreat I was giving in Hawaii. The purpose of the retreat was to explore the interface between spirit, self, and personal healing. One of the key elements of the conference was a daily session focused on understanding dreams.

Jeanine's dreams showed the presence of her cancer and symbolic images of treatments she had received, which included radiation and chemotherapy. In her dreams, an old Victorian-style house with many rooms and hallways symbolized her ravaged body. The house was in disrepair, abandoned, and run down. The halls and rooms were deserted and strewn with black piles of garbage and debris, dream symbols for the cancer itself.

Behind the house was a weed-filled backyard, surrounded by a high fence. The fence had no gate. Beyond the fence lay a beautiful green field, a field she longed to reach in the dream. This was the first dream Jeanine shared with the group.

As time passed during the conference, Jeanine began to look better. Her color changed and she visibly regained a little weight. She and her husband spent happy hours laughing at meals and walking on the beach. We all liked both of them, and we all wanted her to recover. Since part of the conference focused on miraculous healing, we all believed it was possible. Shortly before the conference ended, she had a second dream.

The setting was the same. There was still the old Victorian house and yard, but something had changed. All the trash and debris was gathered up and bagged, placed neatly in the backyard. The house seemed brighter, spruced up. A big change was the addition of a gate in the fence, standing open to the green field beyond. I interpreted the dream as a positive sign that healing and remission had begun. I thought the green field symbolized healing, that the cleanup meant her immune system was beginning to neutralize and absorb the cancer, and that the open gate meant the way was now open to her recovery. How wrong I was!

In truth, this dream was the warning sign of her impending death. That green field, which seemed very attractive and soothing to her in the dream, was the symbol of passage out of life, not into it. The gate stood open—but it was a gateway into another realm of existence. The cleanup was a symbol of inner preparation, getting things in order and preparing her psyche for the transition.

I had lost my objectivity, because I wanted her to live. I interpreted the meaning of the dream as I wanted it to be, a classic trap of interpretation and unconscious projection. I missed the signal. If I had seen it correctly, I could have helped her prepare in a different way for the inevitable result.

Looking and feeling better than she had in years, Jeanine returned home. But her old, habitual patterns of behavior reasserted themselves. Psychically trapped in unhealthy relationships and family-based ideas of how she was "supposed to be," she was unable to make the kinds of changes necessary for recovery. Within a few months, she was dead.

Jeanine taught me that dreams sometimes bring us truth we may not want to hear. She also taught me about the need to step out of ideas about how we want things to be so that we can discover how they really are. If we can accept the message, we may gain insight, peace, and comfort.

A classic dream in psychological literature that signaled the approaching death of a terminally ill patient was recorded by one of the premier Jungian analysts and writers, Marie-Louise Von Franz.[3] It is a good example of this kind of dream.

In the dream the patient, who has been bed ridden and ill, is sitting beside her bed feeling strong and well. Bright sunlight streams through the window of her hospital room. Her doctor tells her she is, "unexpectedly, completely cured," and that she can get dressed and leave. Just as he tells her the good news, she turns around and sees her dead body lying in the bed!

This is really a beautiful dream—the bright sunshine, the feeling of health and strength, the longed-for freedom to leave the hospital—all these things give a pleasant, healing feeling to the dream. When the dreamer sees her dead body in the hospital bed, that is the marker telling us her stay in physical form is ending. Release, light, and healing are contingent on death. Such a dream tells the dreamer it is time to prepare for the transition.

Most people fear death and will resist it even in the face of a terminal diagnosis. Even when illness is painful and destructive, something in us fights to survive. Often, people who are dying have disturbing and frightening dream images, with dream feelings of loss and helplessness. That seems natural, doesn't it? As the psyche struggles to come to grips with the reality of death, we can expect such images to appear in our dreams.

When someone knows they have a terminal diagnosis, it does not necessarily mean they accept it, even if it is accurate and apparently irreversible. In that case, they may get a dream about their death, but the dream images are of others. Perhaps they dream of the death of a close family member or friend. This is an inner projection, an attempt by the ego to deal with the enormity of approaching death by reflecting it outward onto a dream image. Projection means that we "project" unconscious thoughts and perceptions outward onto the screen of our life (or our dreams) where we have a chance to see and understand them. Since the direct view seems too hard to integrate, the dream presents a different screen for viewing.

A twenty-seven year old woman (who died twelve months later) had a dream that illustrates what I mean. She dreamed she went to a movie. In the dream it is an outside, all-night movie. Nighttime often symbolizes the unconscious and unknown parts of something in our dreams. It is "outside," i.e. it is not integrated, not part of her. Suddenly a car pulls up and dumps a dead, pregnant young woman out on the street. The dreamer runs over and knows she is looking at herself lying dead and pregnant, yet at the same time the dead woman doesn't look like her at all.[4]

This is a good example of inner projection—the dead girl is the dreamer but is not her at the same time. It is as if the dreaming consciousness needed to remove the death by one level—from the dreamer to the dream image, yet gives the clue by making her recognize it is she who is lying there.

A powerful symbol in the dream is the pregnancy. Pregnancy is a dream image occurring to many women dealing with terminal illness. I think that is understandable. As a dream symbol pregnancy represents new life, new possibility. There is an element of mystery about pregnancy, just as there is with death. Will the baby be healthy? Will it look like this person or that one? What will he or she be like? Will it be a boy or a girl? Most of these questions will not be answered until the birth. Birth and death are entwined in human experience.

Recognition that our earthly time is drawing to a close is not easily accepted by most of us. Another woman (who died a month later) had a dream of a woman in a department store, wearing a beautiful dress and shoes and carrying a baby. In the dream, she knew that the woman loved the baby "very much."[5] When the dreamer awoke, she felt happy and safe—until she remembered her illness. as she began writing down the dream her fear began again.

The dream brought her a true message of love and safety, relief from the fear she felt over her nearing death. The deep psyche gave her a gift, showing there was nothing to fear. It was only as she returned to her usual way of thinking about it that fear returned. The department store setting is a symbol of potential, of the many possibilities waiting for her. The baby is a symbol of new existence that waits for her after death. The happy woman in the dream is dressed with care, as if for a journey. The context is one of love.

If you really need any motivation to pay attention to dreams, think of this: A dream from the other side can warn us of the possibility of death. If we heed the warning, we might avoid a premature demise. That is especially true when a dream signals the onset of serious illness or disease. Since early diagnosis can make a huge difference in serious illness, the dream can motivate us to get that vital initial physical evaluation that catches trouble in time.

I Can't Go

A woman I grew up with and was best friends with since we were five years old passed away. I had not seen her in years, and when I found out that she was ill, I went to see her. She and I were the same age, our birthdays only two days apart. Our mothers were in the same hospital together when they had us. We were best friends all through grade school and part of high school. She died from breast cancer. I saw her the day before she passed away.

Four years passed and I had a dream about her. She looked great; she was in my driveway with a big station wagon and kept saying, "Come on, come on, let's go." She said, "It's great, you'll love it. I'm soooo happy." I almost went with her, but then I thought of my little girl. I told her, "I can't go right now." I wanted to, but I just said, "I can't go," and walked away.

Very soon after that dream, I was diagnosed with breast cancer. Very odd; it doesn't run in my family and I never really thought about it. I found it immediately. One day the lump

was not there, the next it was. Anyway, I survived my cancer.
It is just a good thing I told her I did not want to go. I came
to find out my surgeon was the same surgeon she had. We were
talking about her when he was doing my biopsy.

I know it was a warning. I'm just glad I told her to come
back another time. I was also glad that she looked so happy.
She left behind two young children. I did not want to do
the same.

That is definitely a warning dream. It is also the kind of
dream that shows us how we can make decisions about our own
death. Her friend is happy on the other side. She looks great,
she's excited—but she's a warning that something is pulling the
dreamer toward death. "Come on, let's go," means leaving life.
This dreamer had more reasons to stay than to leave. If the
dreamer had agreed to go with her friend, I believe she would
have died from the cancer.

When a health dream appears featuring life-threatening illness, it is a wake-up call for the dreamer. Often the dreamer
needs to make difficult and dramatic changes in his or her life if
he or she is to survive. I have worked with many folks in various
stages of illness, including terminal cancer. Sometimes they were
able to get better, because the option to survive was available to
them. They recognized the kind of change needed and had the
courage, desire, and support necessary to make it. Sometimes, as
in the case with Jeanine, they were not able to do so.

It is not always easy to tell the difference between a dream
that uses symbols of illness to address a psychological issue and
one that is talking about the real thing. Cancer, for example, is
a symbol that can appear in a dream as a warning about the
actual disease or as a symptom of internal distress. It is a serious symbol, however we choose to interpret it. I tell people to get
a physical checkup if they dream of having cancer, just to be on
the safe side.

When someone who has passed on appears in a dream and

beckons you to come with them, pay attention. There is no harm intended, but you can bet something serious is taking place in your psyche. After all, this is a symbol of being pulled in some way toward the other side. If you are not ready to go, you had better think of why such a dream might appear. A dream like that is a signal to check out your emotional and physical health. It can also indicate that someone is getting ready to make the transition.

Come for a Walk

I had another dream of my deceased uncle last night. He was beckoning to my mother to come for a walk with him down the street where he used to live. He was walking ahead. (My mother is getting feeble, but she appears far from death's door yet.)

The woman who sent me this dream is psychically sensitive and has had other dreams involving people in her family who have passed on. This dream is setting the stage for her mother's passing. It may be a while yet, but now would be a good time to make sure things are said that need to be said, decisions thought about, and plans made, as might be needed. No one likes planning for death, but if warning is given, it might be a good idea to heed it.

These Dreams Have Got Me Praying

I would like to say that my brother passed away one or two days before this dream, and my father, eleven months before. In the dream, I was sitting on a sofa. I could see my grandma, then my mom, then my stepgrandpa, and then my dad. All of these people passed away in the last six years except my stepgrandfather. He died a long time ago.

Anyway, I saw my stepgrandpa and said, "Hey, Bill," (that was his name), and then my half sister appeared in front of me. She is still alive. She looked a lot younger, like in her thirties. She had on a blue hat with a big sunflower on it. She took my hand and said, "I am dying, and no one knows it yet." I said, "What!" and then I said, "Why are all these people here?" She said something about a mirror and then she went into the kitchen and started to look for something.

I want to talk to all of my kin, so I go back toward the other room. Out of the corner of my eye, I see a white shadow of a figure. I think it is my brother, who passed away a couple of days before. I go into the room and the only person I see is my dad sitting on the floor making a gurgling sound. Then I wake up.

Not long after this, my sister went into the hospital. They said she has a lung disease. They put her on oxygen, and she is using it all the time. This dream happened last year, and she is still doing well.

The dream hasn't affected me much—only that it is telling me she is next to die. I have had other dreams where people passed on that have come true one or two years later. These dreams have got me praying to God to give me more understanding about what they mean.

If I had this dream, I think I would do the best I could to resolve any old bad feelings that might exist between my sister and myself and enjoy her presence while she is still here.

The lineup on the couch of those who have gone before is a symbol supporting the dreamer's thought that her sister is next on the list of family members to die. The lineup certainly suggests a sequence. Of course, the real clincher is the sister's words in the dream: "I am dying, and no one knows it yet." Then a few days later, she is diagnosed with serious lung disease.

How do the dead or the living find a way to communicate to loved ones, through dreams, that death is imminent or that they have entered the final stage of life? It is a mystery of the other side.

At the Banks of the River

•—•··•—•··•··•—•··•—•··•—•··•—•··•—•··•—•··•—•··•—•··•—•··•—•··•··•··•—•·

You Have Twenty-One Years

May I tell you my story? I was diagnosed with breast cancer on December 23, 1997. I spent seven months of 1998 going through chemo, surgery, and radiation. Thanks to wonderful support, I am now cancer-free.

A couple of months before the diagnosis, I had a dream that I remembered quite well and discussed with my husband the next day. I thought the dream meant that I had twenty-one years to live and I did not like the idea of dying at age seventy-four. After the diagnosis, of course, it was an encouragement to me, although I still want more time than that.

Here is what happened in the dream: I walked into the post office to mail Christmas presents to my family. The post office was packed with people during the Christmas rush. I noticed a black man sitting on a stool in the middle of a crowd. Everyone seemed to be asking him for some piece of information. I walked over toward him. There were a few people between us, but I easily had his full attention. He asked me my name and I told him. He then said, "You have twenty-one years." The dream ended.

Talking with a friend, we decided the dream was metaphorical, meaning I would have plenty of time. Later, I thought, time to become more mature—twenty-one: the age of arrival.

There isn't any way to know exactly what this dream means, except that it predated the cancer diagnosis and indicated time was available. A dream presenting specific numbers in regard to years of life is tricky, because numbers are symbols just like everything else in a dream. One thing, though, is that such a dream definitely can help take the edge off a diagnosis of serious illness. You may be ill, but the dream says your time is not yet up.

The black figure is a symbol of a deep, unconscious wisdom that knows the truth about the dreamer. Everyone is asking him something. "Everyone" is a symbol of the many facets of the dreamer's inner self. We all have a figure like this inside us, and it can appear to us in our dreams to warn or advise us.

Did you notice that the dreamer is not comfortable with the idea she may have only twenty-one years left? Even a hint of the timing of our death is disturbing, yet we all come to the river eventually. If I had this dream, I would not necessarily take it to mean I had only twenty-one years to live, but I would also pay close attention to the end of that period, if I was still around. When this dreamer turns seventy-four, perhaps she will remember the dream and live life as if she was walking in the shadow of death. To live life as if each day is the last is a powerful teaching.

The concept of death as a friend and powerful teacher is not popular. We go to great lengths to deny the reality of death, but our denial will not change reality. Without getting obsessive about things, I feel it is a good idea for us to contemplate the truth of our death from time to time. It gives us an opportunity to ask ourselves if there is anything we want to change about how we are living our life. That can lead to some interesting discoveries, even renewal in the here and now.

We are all rather stubborn about changing things, even in the face of death. We get set in our ways. It takes a real look beyond the veil to get our attention and force us to change our way of thinking. That is one gift a dream from the other side can bring to us.

One of the most famous dreams foreshadowing physical death came to Abraham Lincoln. About two weeks before Lincoln fell to his assassin's bullet, he had a dream, documented in Carl Sandburg's biography of Lincoln.[6] One night as he slept, Lincoln seemed to awaken to the sounds of people sobbing and crying. In his dream, he got up and went downstairs. He wandered through the White House, seeking the source of the sounds. He entered the East Room and saw a corpse dressed in funeral clothing lying there, guarded by soldiers. The face of the corpse was hidden—Lincoln could not see who it was. Many people surrounded the casket.

Lincoln asked one of the soldiers, "Who is dead in the White House?" The soldier answered, "The President. He was killed by an assassin." Loud sobbing from the crowd of people woke him from the dream.

As you can imagine, this dream greatly disturbed Lincoln. Things were hard for him at the time. His wife was not emotionally stable, the Civil War had ended with half the nation in ruins, postwar politics was asserting itself with a vengeance, and Lincoln himself was physically and mentally exhausted. Lincoln said of his dream, "I slept no more that night: and although it was only a dream, I have been strangely annoyed by it ever since."[7]

Two weeks later, the president's body lay on a bier raised in the East Room of the White House.

Other famous people have had dreams and visions of their death. Carl Jung gave the world analytical psychology, a way of looking at the human psyche that ventures into the realm of the soul. Jung was one of the great thinkers of the twentieth century, unique in his contribution to psychology and the understanding of the human spirit. He was quite psychic and had many dreams that pierced the barrier between here and the other side. Dreams are an integral part of his work and the work of contemporary Jungian therapists.

In 1944, Jung almost died of a heart attack. While the issue of his survival was still in doubt, he experienced a powerful vision. He found himself far above the earth, approaching a sacred temple, eager to rejoin a group of people with whom he belonged. He was on the verge of understanding what his life had meant, what his purpose had been, and why he had taken earthly existence. Just as these things were about to be revealed, he was distracted by an image of his doctor rising from the earth far below. In a kind of telepathic exchange, the doctor informed Jung that it was not time to leave and that he must return.

That was the end of the vision, and Jung says that it took three weeks for him to make up his mind to live again. He tells the story in his book, *Memories, Dreams, Reflections*.[8]

Jung also realized that the doctor's life was in jeopardy and tried to warn him. Jung's understanding of the mystical and spiritual was far beyond average, and he sensed that the nature of the vision was dangerous to the doctor's health. The doctor, of course, refused to give credence to Jung's warning, or even to discuss the vision experience. Sure enough, as Jung began to recover, the doctor fell ill and soon died.[9]

Jung's recovery was marked by extraordinary visions that gave him a new sense of his impersonal and objective self. The visions and dreams taught him detachment in a way nothing else could have accomplished, and bore fruit afterward in the creation of some of his most important works.

Once Jung had a dream of someone like his wife dying and rising up from a gravelike pit, wearing a gown of white inscribed with strange symbols. He awoke, noting it was three in the morning, and thought to himself that the dream signaled someone's death. The next day he learned a cousin of his wife had died the night before—at three in the morning.[10]

Jung thought that life after death would pick up at about the same place where life before death left off—with the same level of spiritual and psychological development available to the individual that was present before death. Not so different, really, from the ancient Greeks and their vision of the Elysian fields.

Unlike the Greeks, Jung foresaw ongoing development for the soul, which would pursue learning and understanding that had escaped it on earth. Some months before his mother's unexpected death, Jung had a dream of his father, who had died over a quarter of a century before. It was the first dream he had of his father in all that time. In the dream, his father wanted to talk about marital psychology, since Jung was a psychologist.

Jung awoke. In hindsight, he later understood that this dream presaged his mother's death. His father wanted to know how to deal with the problems of marriage. Jung took this to mean that he was still unenlightened in the afterlife regarding marital relations, and wanted to gain insight since he knew that the relationship was about to be renewed.[11]

I don't know if Jung is right, and that we continue on much as before, with the same mental and perceptual limitations we hold at death. I do not think it is possible for us to conceive of being very different from who we are, leaving aside fantasy and role playing. It makes sense that if we think about our existence after death, we will tend to frame that existence in terms and feelings familiar to us in life. What else can we do? We have nothing to compare it to, nothing upon which we can base our ideas except centuries of myth, fable, superstition, and cultural bias. In the end, we will all discover the truth and the mystery will be revealed. Until that time, we may look upon our dreams as one of the ways to catch a glimpse of what lies in the undiscovered country.

Chapter 6

Reincarnation

The soul is ever free; it is deathless because it is birthless.
Man is *a soul and* has *a body.*

—PARAMAHANSA YOGANANDA

IT IS NOT POSSIBLE to talk about the other side without running head on into one of the most fascinating and controversial subjects of all—reincarnation. Reincarnation is the idea that our souls return to this physical world sometime after we die, in a new and different body. My experience with the Angel of Death as a column of pure, red light in 1975 convinced me that physical death was not the end. A series of unexpected and spontaneous past-life memories in 1977 convinced me we have lived before.

SPONTANEOUS MEMORIES

One day I was sitting in a friend's kitchen, talking with her about nothing in particular, when I felt an irresistible compulsion to close my eyes and quiet myself. As soon as I did, I found myself transported to an ancient plain, surrounded by the chaos of war. A horrendous battle was taking place. It was hot. The air stank of the smell of blood. I could feel and see my body. I was shorter, stockier. My skin was darker. I was dressed in a leather breastplate, plainly decorated with embossed metal. I wore a short skirt of leather strips with a kind of leather undergarment beneath it and carried a sword in my right hand, a shield in my left. I knew that I was somewhere near Greece. I knew that I was the equivalent of a sergeant, a squad leader of some sort.

Men were screaming and fighting all about me. I could see a terrible war chariot thundering toward me, sunlight flashing off wicked, spinning knives on the wheels. I could see the charioteer, angry and dark, his helmet shaped like a beehive. Then something struck me hard with a sharp and terrible pain. I fell to the ground, and as I fell the chariot wheel passed over me and crushed me to death. I gasped out loud and clutched my chest, startled back to ordinary awareness in that ordinary kitchen, on what was no longer an ordinary day. I *felt* that spear strike me; I *felt* that chariot roll over me. Across the table, my friend was looking at me very oddly.

That was the first of several unsolicited memories of past lives that took place over about a few months' time. Years later, regression work brought other memories to the surface, but this time of spontaneous discovery was a remarkable and disturbing experience, all the more so because it was not sought for. During the same time period that I was having these past-life memories, I was exploring healing work and becoming far more sensitive to the subtle energies that surround us and make up an integral part of our existence. The spontaneous memories and the discoveries I was making about healing energetics seemed to me somehow related.

The next past-life memory I had came two days later. It was of Anne, the same woman sitting at the kitchen table when the first memory surfaced, and myself. At the time, she and I were intimately involved in an on again, off again kind of relationship. Anne was very psychic, a true sensitive—perhaps that is why these things began in her presence. In the new memory, I found myself again back in an ancient time. Neither Anne nor I looked as we did in this life, but I knew it was her. In this past life, anxious to get me out of the way to make room for a lover, she poisoned me! You can probably imagine our conversations about that memory.

A day later, another memory of Anne, another life, another appearance of the soul in a different body. This time, we were dancing outdoors at night on a stone-paved patio, under a summer sky. Suddenly the ground began to tremble and shake. I could hear an eerie sound that grew louder by the second. It sounded like nothing I have ever heard in this life, and it had a deathly, deafening roar and crashing to it. An enormous wave appeared, looming high against the stars. In an instant we were overwhelmed and drowned.

Ever since I remembered this scene, I have thought that dance floor of stone still exists somewhere on the bottom of the ocean, covered with the debris of millennia, along with the rest of fabled Atlantis.

Many times, it seems, I have been a soldier. It also seems we bring with us the skills and abilities learned in our past lives. When I was nine years old, I began collecting guns. I don't mean toy guns. I mean the real thing, antique pistols and rifles from the American past. I mowed lawns and ran errands to earn the money. Fascinated by weapons, I spent hours fantasizing about their history. I felt eerily familiar with the pistols and rifles from the Civil War era. By the time I was twelve, I had quite a collection. Old guns were a lot cheaper and a lot more plentiful then.

When I turned twelve, I joined a gun club, sponsored by two friendly adults who regularly picked me up and took me to the range. Everyone expected kids like me to take a while to learn the ins and outs of gun safety and accurate shooting. For me, there wasn't any breaking-in period. I knew immediately what to do—how to handle guns safely and how to shoot them with fine accuracy.

The gun club was affiliated with the NRA, a somewhat different organization in 1953 than it is today. The NRA had a marksmanship program for young shooters up to sixteen years of age, designed to produce accurate marksmen and point the way toward competition shooting. The program was long and complex, progressing through different degrees of difficulty, based on scores and shooting positions. Each level upward was marked by a name, a medal, and a cloth patch that could be sewn onto a shooting jacket. The program began at "pro-marksman" and ended, many targets and levels later, at "distinguished rifleman." It was not unusual to take a year or two to complete the entire cycle, and most never did. It was not easy to get that highest award.

I was different. I shot the whole thing in two weeks, just shooting each level, taking down the targets, and moving to the next. The adult instructors could not believe that a twelve-year-old beginner was blowing through a year's progression in such a short time. It still took a long time to get all my patches, because the rules said you could shoot only one level a week at the fastest pace. The club would send in my targets once a week for each succeeding level, to comply with the regulations. How did I know how to shoot so well at twelve years old?

In 1977, soon after the memory of the tidal wave, I found myself caught up in another past-life experience, perched on a limb in a grove of trees. It was morning on a sunny day, mist rising from the ground. I had a long and elegant single-shot rifle with a telescope in my hands, and I was looking out over a civil war battlefield toward the Union lines. I knew I was near a town called Sharpsburg. My uniform was a dirty gray. I was a sharp-shooter in the Confederate Army.

Years later, I learned that the Battle of Sharpsburg was what the Union forces called the Battle of Antietam, one of the blood-iest slaughters of the entire Civil War. A famous part of the engagement took place in a grove of trees where many died, including several Confederate sharpshooters. And, yes, I remember the bullet that struck and killed me in that lifetime.

I never had to think twice about how to shoot a rifle, and shoot it well. After that past-life memory, I knew why.

I am disturbed and moved by stories of the Civil War. I saw the incredible Ken Burns video documentary on the war and found myself crying for those men lying bloated and stiff in those old, scratched, and faded pictures, among their ruined wagons and dead horses. I feel compassion for the dead of other wars and other times, but thinking of the War Between the States always evokes sadness and deep emotional pain.

I have other memories of war and battle in past times and dis-tant lands. At least this time around I did not have to go into combat. My service with the Marine Corps ended in 1964, so I never had to face the horrors of Vietnam. Could it be I have learned whatever was needed about war and a soldier's life? I certainly hope so.

Learning seems to be the point of reincarnation. Sometimes it is not at all clear what the lesson is supposed to be, although it is always about love and compassion in some way. Another mem-ory I have is of a dreary and joyless life as a woman on the American plains sometime during the late 1800s. Drudgery, poverty, sickness, and an early death are what I remember of that life. What lesson can I take from that? I don't know—per-haps a lesson of compassion for the pain of the human condition. Perhaps I can express a deeper understanding, a deeper com-passion for others, because I know on some level what it is like to live that kind of life.

You can see from the personal stories I have shared with you that I am a firm believer in reincarnation. Of course it is possible to think of different explanations for what I experienced, ranging from outright psychopathology to vivid imagination. The only trouble with those explanations is that I am not mentally ill, hallucinatory, or subject to overwhelming bouts of unreality through daydreams or imagination. And what was it that compelled me to close my eyes on that afternoon back in 1977?

REINCARNATION AND KARMA

Reincarnation is a favorite target for skeptics of all kinds, as is the content of most of this book. Near-death experiences, visitations and messages from beyond the veil, spirits and angels—all these and more are brushed off as fantasy or wishful thinking. I have an answer for all of these folks, but it won't prove anything to them or change their minds. My answer is simply this: We will all find out the truth when we die. Until then, we are free to believe what we will, based on our life's journey and the events that happen along the way. I would not have it any other way.

The idea of reincarnation has been around for a very long time. It is not an idea well understood in the West, nor is its companion doctrine of karma, the law of spiritual cause and effect. In the East, reincarnation and karma are the cornerstones of the two great religions of Buddhism and Hinduism.

Free will is a concept basic to the doctrine of karma. Karma is misunderstood in the West as fate. "Fate" is a word that implies inevitability about something. Implicit in the concept of fate is a lack of any possibility of changing the situation or altering the effect. If it is "fated," we are helpless victims of unseen and irresistible cosmic forces. Fate by necessity reduces us to petitioning unseen and divine powers for change, since we cannot ourselves bring about the results we desire. We disempower ourselves and give away the very thing that could see us through, our freedom to choose how we will respond to the events of our lives and our deaths.

Karma, on the other hand, gives back the power. We are not victims of an inexorable fate but are free to shape and change the events and results of our lives, now and in lives to come. We release karma built up by past action by learning the lesson, whatever it may be, and acting accordingly in the present. We are free to learn, to grow, and to choose paths that lead us to spiritual realization and evolution as conscious beings. Inevitably, we arrive at a path of service and recognition of the reality of love as the basis for all things.

Karma is the result of the choices we make. Understanding karma means recognizing that all things, all actions, all thoughts compose a dynamic and living matrix of timeless existence, and that all things interact and affect one another. What we put out returns to us in one way or another, and what we offer to others through our presence is part of their learning as well. Karma is not about retribution or punishment for past misdeeds, as it is often presented. It is a description of spiritual law, and it is our own choice whether to accept responsibility for our actions or not. Reincarnation is a way for us to learn that lesson and come full circle back to where we started—in love and compassion.

THE CHRISTIAN CONTROVERSY

In the West, reincarnation was once a common idea. In the early years of Christianity, the best known proponent of reincarnation as part of Christian doctrine was Origen of Alexandria, who died about 250 C.E., a martyr in the faith. It does not take much thought to realize that belief in reincarnation is in conflict with some of the most fundamental tenets of orthodox Christian theology. If we are born again into the physical world, how can we also credit the idea of hellfire and eternal punishment (or reward)? What happens to the idea of resurrection of the physical body on the final Day of Judgment? Most of all, if we reincarnate, what happens to the very idea of Christian salvation? From a Christian point of view, this is the ultimate heresy—perhaps it is no longer necessary to accept Christ as the only way of return to God. It is no surprise that the whole idea of reincarnation found no favor with the early rulers of the church. The Second Council of Constantinople in 553 officially condemned the doctrine of reincarnation (and Origen's work) as anathema.

There are several passages in the Bible, though, that seem to indicate that Christ himself talked of reincarnation. Here are two, taken from the King James Version.

> *For all the prophets and the law prophesied until John. And if ye will receive it, he is Elias, which was for to come.*
> *—Matthew 11:13–14*

> *And his disciples asked him, saying, Why then say the scribes that Elias must first come? And Jesus answered and said unto them, Elias truly shall first come, and restore all things. But I say unto you, That Elias is come already, and they knew him not, but have done unto him whatsoever they listed. Likewise shall also the Son of man suffer of them. Then the disciples understood that he spake unto them of John the Baptist.*
> *—Matthew 17:10–13*

People have argued over the meaning of this passage for centuries. To me it looks like Jesus is saying that the spirit comes again in physical form.

THE CATHARS

The final death knell for organized Western belief in reincarnation came with the suppression of the Cathars in the thirteenth century. A large and prosperous Christian religious community, the Cathars controlled what is now Burgundy in southern France. They had an elaborate belief system formulated in gnostic Christian communities during the earliest days of the faith. The Cathars believed women were equally qualified to serve as leaders and celebrants of the mass with the men. They also believed in having a direct relationship with God, requiring neither church nor priest to act as intercessor. That alone would have made them targets for the zealots of the Church, along with belief in reincarnation.

Unfortunately for the Cathars, both the king of France and the Italian pope eyed the rich farmlands and resources of Burgundy. The king wanted control of the lands; the pope wanted the revenues that would come to the Church as a result of French control. In 1209, Pope Innocent the Third declared a crusade. Known as the Albigensian Crusade (because the Cathars lived in the region of Albi), it was the last crusade. Under the guise of exterminating heresy, the armies sent against the Cathars slaughtered them to the last man, woman, and child. It took years, but when it was over, the consolidation of control in Europe by the church was complete and absolute. The subject of reincarnation became a nonissue. For most of the West, things remained that way for another seven hundred years or so.

BRIDEY MURPHY

Move forward to the twentieth century, and in 1952 we encounter the story of Bridey Murphy. Probably more than anything else, this controversial story served to reawaken general interest in the West in reincarnation.

A hypnotherapist named Morey Bernstein was working with a woman named Virginia Tighe. During one of their sessions, she began speaking with an Irish accent and claiming (under hypnosis) to be someone named Bridey Murphy from County Cork,

Ireland, a woman who had lived a hundred years in the past. Bernstein wrote a book about the case called *The Search for Bridey Murphy*, published in 1956. A worldwide sensation, the book brought both skeptics and believers out in droves. Whether the past-life memories of Ms. Tighe were genuine has never been satisfactorily determined. The book seeded a widespread reintroduction of the concept of reincarnation to the Western world.

THE DALAI LAMA

You have probably heard of the Dalai Lama, the exiled spiritual leader of Tibet, who now lives in Northern India. In the Tibetan tradition, great teachers reincarnate many times as part of their service to humanity. Each incarnation carries the wisdom and experience of the past lives of that particular teacher. After the physical death of a teacher, a search begins according to pre-scribed, traditional methods for the new body occupied by his (or her) reincarnated soul.

The search for the current Dalai Lama began in 1933. The regent of Tibet received a vision and a dream indicating where the monks should look for their new leader. Clear details and specific information about his home and surroundings were provided. In 1937, the searchers found a young boy who matched all the criteria. At the age of two, he spoke the dialect of central Tibet (not the region where he was born). He identified the disguised monks correctly for who they were and without hesitation picked out personal items belonging to his predecessor from other similar items laid before him. His home and surroundings accurately matched the vision and dream that led the monks to his side. Many other well-documented stories attest to the reality of the current Dalai Lama's knowledge of previous lives.

EDGAR CAYCE

One of the great stories of the twentieth century is the story of Edgar Cayce. Cayce could accurately diagnose illness at a distance while in a deep trance and was able to prescribe effective cures without ever seeing the patient in person. When in his normal waking state, he never recalled anything said in his trance "sleep." Cayce was the genuine article, never profiting from his amazing ability or seeking the fame and attention thrust upon him. In the end, his dedication to service and his inability to turn away the people who sought his help compromised his health and led to his death.

Cayce came from a traditional southern Christian background and was a strong believer in conventional ideas about God and spirit. You can imagine his waking discomfort when told he had been speaking about the past lives of some of his patients during the trance state. These descriptions of past existence would occur in context with the health or counseling readings he was giving. Perhaps a present illness had its roots in a past-life experience, or a troublesome circumstance could be traced back to a previous incarnation.

To make matters worse, some of his patients had past lives that took place on the lost continent of Atlantis. Cayce described an elaborate Atlantean civilization in some of his readings, and affirmed that many Atlantean souls were reincarnating at the time. This was before and during World War II. Cayce saw the events leading up to war partly as a continuation of the lessons these ancient Atlantean souls needed to complete or learn.

For Cayce, the real lesson was always about love, acceptance, and the embrace of God. The lessons of any past life referred back to the underlying theme of compassion and service. Cayce also set great store in dreams, both as vehicles for understanding and resolving troubling personal issues, and as doorways to the other side, windows onto existence after death.

Cayce was quite sure that dreams were powerful vehicles for talking with the other side. In his terminology, when asleep, the soul was free to communicate with the "subconscious minds of those whether in the material or cosmic plane."[12] In other words, when we sleep, the door opens for connection to those who have gone on. Many of Cayce's readings emphasized that all was well on the other side. Friends, family, and others who had gone on were happy, healthy, and aware of the events taking place with their loved ones here on the physical plane.

I have a friend who has dedicated her life to spirit and service. Eleanor is an intuitive sensitive and receives guidance and advice through dreams and visions. She has written several books about her experiences. She shared this dream with me, and this seems like the place to put it, since it features Edgar Cayce in a dream of return.

Cayce Comes to Visit

In 1988, I was spending a lot of time giving comfort and counsel to friends who were having relationship and financial problems. I was loaning money to friends in need and urging them to visualize abundance. I told a number of people about a process for gaining abundance, where you set a crystal wineglass or a silver chalice or tumbler on your home meditation altar. I instructed them to write a clear, concise sentence or two about their financial needs and to visualize the funds in hand as they placed the piece of paper in the chalice.

"Remember," I told them, "set the chalice and the intention for manifestation. You deserve abundance." Meanwhile my own funds were dwindling as a result of my generosity with the many people who had come to me in need. Still, it never occurred to me to ask for supply for myself since I have always had enough.

One night as I lay peacefully sleeping, a figure appeared in a dream. I instantly recognized him as Edgar Cayce, a lifelong source of inspiration to me. Cayce stood before me, smiling kindly, and told me one need not have shame or guilt about having money. Money is merely a tool or a resource. Sufficient money is our birthright. His eyes blazed and he said, with great authority, "Now, with all your help to others, SET THE CHALICE FOR YOURSELF!"

He had been watching me dole out funds and urging others to take responsibility for increase and supply. He knew of the "Chalice Experiment" we were practicing. Finally, he knew I was not taking heed of my own finances and could be a more convincing mentor and counselor if I had personal experience and testimony to share about using thought to create abundance. I went to a store that sold fine china and bought a silver goblet. Mentally thanking dear Edgar Cayce, I wrote out my affirmation of supply and placed it in the silver chalice.

Shortly after, I was given a dream to start my own company, creating inspirational books and tapes. Since then I have been richly blessed in countless ways, with a large country acreage, speaking trips to seven countries, media interviews, and thirty trips around the world. But most of all, I've been given a peaceful mind and a thankful heart and a loving circle of family and friends with whom to share them.

I don't know why the spiritual universe includes reincarnation. I know what everyone says about it, and I know what people who return from the other side in dreams say about it. One thing consistent through all of the teachings, from whatever source, is the idea of learning about love and compassion. We seem to be in a very confusing, very mysterious school for the soul. Our job on Earth is to learn the lessons and apply them.

Eleanor shared another dream with me that illustrates the point. Remember, the dead have to follow the rules of dreams, which means they communicate in dreams with the symbols of dream language. We see a symbol that we can understand, but it does not necessarily mean our loved ones on the other side are doing exactly what appears in the dream. What counts is the essence of the message.

Dad Returns to Thank Me

In August of 1988, my father died of a brain tumor. We had a close relationship and his death was a blow to the entire family. One aspect of grace for me, however, was that I accepted his death and knew he was on the other side.

The day he left his body (in Reston, Virginia), I was driving my car along a six-lane highway in Denver, Colorado. Suddenly, he appeared in my car and said, "Honey, I'm going to be leaving soon and wanted to say good-bye."

I was so shocked at the unexpected appearance of a ghost in my car, even though it was my beloved father, that I reacted by yanking the steering wheel to the left. My car careened across three lanes of oncoming traffic to the opposite side of the highway.

Somehow I avoided colliding with the other cars and was able to turn the car in the proper direction and drive to an exit ramp, where I sat panting and staring off into space for several minutes. Later that night, my father left his body in Hospice, after having had no food or drink for eight days. He had been a kind, courageous, generous, religious man all of his life. But he had told the visiting priest assigned to Hospice that he just couldn't let go of his body because he was afraid he should have done more with his life and that perhaps he would go to hell!

A short time after his death, he came to me in a dream. I could see a university setting behind him and noticed he was carrying textbooks. He was wearing a yellow knit shirt and white slacks, like the golf clothes he often wore when playing golf on the weekends. He looked very young and healthy and was radiant. He started the conversation by doing something uncharacteristic. He jumped up and down on the grass several times to make his point.

Reincarnation

He said, *"Look! See how healthy and energetic I am? I am in great shape and very busy, so I can't stay long. I'm on my way to a class. You were always telling me about reincarnation and karma, remember? And I pooh-poohed it and made jokes about it since I had stayed in the Catholic Church. I just didn't see where all those beliefs could fit into my faith. But, Honey, you were right."*

Gratitude seemed to extend itself from every pore in his body toward me. "The irony is that now I'm over here having to go to school to learn all of the things that you tried to tell me for years. I just wanted to let you know that it's really beautiful over here and that I'm healthier and happier than I've ever been. You were right all along. I love you, Honey. I have to go now—to my class." He laughed his characteristic jubilant laugh, waved, and was gone.

I awoke with a feeling of deep gratitude that he was happy and had found challenging and fulfilling new studies to help him make sense of our sojourn on Earth. As I sat up in bed, it was as if a heavy overcoat slipped from my shoulders. It seemed like some ancient thought of being misunderstood, ridiculed, or rejected for my spiritual beliefs peeled itself from my aura and evaporated. I was free at last from wanting the approval of my father.

Eleanor saw her father in a university setting, carrying textbooks. I don't think it is actually like that on the other side (I could be wrong!), but I think those are perfect symbols to convey the essence of what her father is doing there—learning and expanding his spiritual understanding. What I love about this story is the release of old thought patterns of wanting parental approval. That is the kind of marker signaling a true dream of return.

GENERAL GEORGE S. PATTON

Many famous people have experienced some form of past-life recognition or memory. General George S. Patton is a well-known example. In many ways the epitome of a professional soldier, Patton was noted for his belief in reincarnation. He was convinced he had been to war many times in previous lives and had served in the armies of Alexander the Great and ancient Rome. He knew things about the terrain and locale of his campaigns in Africa and Europe impossible to understand except by previous knowledge. Explosive, arrogant, and temperamental, he was a soldier's soldier, living and breathing a harsh and somewhat archaic code of war that led him to great heights and great humiliations. He would have been more at home in Caesar's legions than in the "democratic" American Army of World War II.

TAYLOR CALDWELL

Another interesting example is Taylor Caldwell, the famous novelist who authored *Dear and Glorious Physician* and several other well-known works. She was one of the most successful writers of her time. A skeptic at first, she discovered many past-life experiences. Caldwell's past-life memories are recorded in a book by Jess Stearn,[13] who also wrote a best-selling work about Edgar Cayce.

Caldwell recalled several previous lifetimes under hypnosis. They included memories as a student of the Greek physician Hippocrates, a life as a princess of the Incas, and one life as a maid in the household of Mary Ann Evans, who wrote under the pseudonym of George Eliot. Taylor Caldwell's novels reflect a broad knowledge of the practice of medicine and the feeling of daily life in the world of biblical times. That would not be unusual, except for the fact that she never actually studied that historical period.

I am not the only one who has decided after initial doubt that past lives are real. One well-known proponent of past-life existence is Brian Weiss, M.D. Dr. Weiss is the former Chief of Psychiatry at Mt. Sinai Medical Center in Miami, Florida. His credentials in the medical community are impeccable. He has written several successful books, including *Many Lives, Many Masters* and *Through Time Into Healing*. Dr. Weiss found himself in the interesting position of having a client unexpectedly enter a past-life experience under hypnosis. In time, this led to a cure for her problems, issues that had resisted conventional therapy. He has become a national and articulate champion for past-life therapy as a vehicle for present healing.

Dr. Weiss relates stories of people losing large amounts of weight, cures of various illnesses, improved relationships, and other desirable results. Whenever I focus on past-life therapy in my own practice, I see confirmation of what he has so thoroughly documented—results, dramatic and real. That is what matters most to me as a therapist. Past-life therapy offers possibilities for genuine healing that other approaches may not be able to address.

People come to my office for many reasons, but everyone has something that he or she is trying to work out or change in his or her life. It can take a lot of time in therapeutic sessions to get to the bottom of things and evoke the inner process of healing and resolution. Past-life hypnotic regression can sometimes be a powerful, rapid, and highly effective way to work with emotional, physical, and spiritual problems. Tapping into a past-life experience where present-day problems may be rooted can lead to dramatic results and improvement. It holds the potential for understanding and integrating difficulties in the present.

I have not performed anywhere near as many past-life regressions as Dr. Weiss has, but I can say with certainty that something is going on here beyond what we usually think about life after death.

A CASE HISTORY

Here is an example from one of my clients, used by permission. She is a professional woman just turned thirty, with two young children. Brittany has returned to college and is studying psychology. She is Caucasian and comes from a Christian background. She is also a psychic sensitive, meaning she is able to accurately sense information about people not available in usual ways.

Brittany wanted to gain some insight into a health problem and thought that a past-life regression might provide some helpful information. She proved to be a responsive hypnotic subject with good visualization abilities. When I took her through the doorway to the past, she emerged in a horrendous and traumatic situation.

Brittany found herself in the body of an infant, thrown into a pit with her mother, wrapped in a black and airless body bag. Her mother was dead, but the infant that Brittany had become in memory was still alive and suffocating in the bag.

In my office, Brittany gasped and struggled, crying as she described what she was feeling. I guided her to a place where she could detach from the feelings and suffering, becoming an observer of the scene. She felt that the event took place in Europe, during the period leading up to World War II. She and her mother, along with many others, were murdered by the Nazis and buried in a mass grave.

During this same session, Brittany described another past life as a young African girl in some undefined place and time. Here is a note she wrote about her memories. What is interesting is that she points out one of the controversial areas open to question regarding past-life regressions and memories. I think it is important to examine these kinds of memories with care, although I am convinced past lives are a reality.

Reincarnation

I Felt Overwhelmed

I don't know if I mentioned this last week, but I wrote a short story when I was in middle school about the journey of a young tribal girl. She did not like to be referred to as feminine, but was named so. She performed a duty for her tribe (as a messenger in a dangerous situation) and was renamed for her bravery.

I haven't been able to locate the paper yet, which is somewhere in the recesses of my basement. Her new name started with a T and reminded me of the name I was trying to grasp in the life I experienced under hypnosis. Of course, then comes the question of did I "remember" the name from part of my subconscious and use it in my story, or did I remember it from my story and place it in my regression?

I saw more detail than I cared to explain during the regression, and I felt overwhelmed by having to tell you what I saw. At the time I had to struggle to tell you what I was experiencing, because I was more focused on just taking it in than relaying it to you. The first regression experience was so draining that it was difficult to move on freely to the others. It would be interesting to visit other lives without so much trauma to begin with. I definitely tune in to the emotion and find it hard to disconnect.

I don't know if the name in the story came from Brittany's subconscious memory of a past life or if the past-life memory of a name came from the story. It can be argued that past-life memories are simply fictions created by the subconscious for a variety of reasons. We each have to come to our own conclusion, but for me there is no doubt about the reality of reincarnation.

Brittany's trouble describing what she saw is not uncommon. That is often true when the memory is traumatic and disturbing. Not all past-life memories are like this, but there is always the possibility of tapping into a painful experience. Brittany also shared a story with me about her three-year-old son. Children often talk about things that sound like memories of past lives. The memories usually fade as the child grows older. The window onto the other side closes with age.

Remember When I Was Big Like Daddy?

My son, Michael, woke up early one morning (before dawn) when he was two and a half. He came into my room and was still a bit out of it. He said, "Mommy, remember when I was big like Daddy and I crashed the car and I went to the hospital where the doctor put screws in my knees?" I told him I didn't remember and asked him if I was there. He said yes. I asked if I was sad. He said, "No, you knew I'd be okay." I then tried to pursue this, but he very quickly changed the subject to "Can I watch cartoons?" Ever since then, he has complained about his knees.

Some pain is probably from growing pains. But he even tells me to slow down when I am walking with him because it will hurt his knees. (He is now three and a half). He wakes up in the middle of the night crying and won't calm down until I tell him his knees are well and I rub them for him.

I contacted a woman via the Internet who wrote a book about children's recollections of past lives. She agreed that he might be recalling one. Okay, I've bent your ear long enough.

Age is not a factor in reincarnation. What incarnates again is the soul, the ageless essence of being. Whether we die young or old, the essence of who we are remains immortal and unaffected by physical death. That means it is possible to meet again in this physical lifetime someone who has gone before.

Reincarnation

I Had a Knowing

My child, a girl, died at six months of age in a crib death. I had a knowing that she would return as one of my son's children.

When my son's middle child was about three, we were together in the washroom doing chores and I sat him on a counter while I was busy. I turned around and he was sobbing. I said, "Honey . . . what is the matter?" He said, "Bobbi, I don't want to have to die again!"

I told him we are all going to die, it is nothing to fear . . . but I promised him this time he would live to be a very old man. He calmed down and did not speak of it again.

People can have dreams of their past lives, or at least dreams that certainly seem to reflect past lives. A dream of a past life is very different from a regular dream. Like genuine dreams of return, there is a different feeling and quality to the dream.

Dreams of past lives feel very real. All dreams feel real, but these are more like waking life than like a dream. Often, there is no particular message that is obvious to interpretation. One woman had dreams of walking down a narrow cobbled street in a foreign city, perhaps near the end of the nineteenth century. She remembers a feeling of poverty, cold, and hunger, sharing food (but not enough) in a dreary, dark room after a day of weary labor.

What can we make of that? This is not a normal kind of dream. I should know—I have discussed and listened to literally thousands of dreams over the past twenty years or so, and dreams are usually not like this. What stands out is the complete absence of any typical dream events, like rapid shifts to a different scene or action, or the appearance of dream elements that seem incongruent with the actions or setting. The dream of walking down the street is different. So is this next dream.

It Was Hard to Breathe

I was five years old and in a shower room with a lot of people. We all had very short hair and the room was lined with tile. There were large tin showerheads in the room, and we were naked. There were so many people in the room that it was hard to breathe. Then we all went to sleep!

The woman who told me this says she is haunted by the dream. Where were people with short hair crowded naked into "showers," and put to "sleep"? This is not the first dream or story I have heard that seems to reflect the mass murders in the extermination camps of World War II. It appears that at least some of the victims have returned.

When I first sat down to write this book, it was not my intention to include anything about reincarnation. I found that it just wasn't possible for me to talk about the other side, given my personal experiences, and not bring it up. We continue on after death. We return again, if there is more we need to learn. Judging from all those memories, I must be a slow student!

Chapter 7

━━━━━━━━━━━━━━━━━━━━━━━━━━━━━━━━━━━━

Parting the Veil

━━━━━━━━━━━━━━━━━━━━━━━━━━━━━━━━━━━━

Nothing before, nothing behind.
The steps of faith fall on the seeming void
And find the rock beneath.
　　　　　—JOHN GREENLEAF WHITTIER

MANY PEOPLE WOULD LIKE TO HAVE just one more chance to talk with someone who has crossed over to the other side. Every society has ideas about death and the afterlife, including ideas about parting the veil and reconnecting to the dead. Many cultures avoid any attempt to contact the other side out of fear the spirits of the dead will be angry or malevolent, bringing bad luck and ill will.

In our society, traditional thoughts about the other side are changing. Many popular shows on television feature mediums and psychics who claim to be in touch with the dead. Are they tuned in to the other side? It's not for me to say, but many seem convinced that a connection is being made. From stories of ghost busters to serious researchers of the paranormal, any given night's viewing is likely to provide an opportunity for watching something eerie. We are all fascinated by the mysterious and by tales of the other side.

There are many ways to go about establishing contact, and some of those are available to you, if you want to try. There is a catch: It is important to realize that the power of the unconscious mind can easily confuse the issue. The desire to believe can definitely get in the way of genuine experience. In this chapter, I want to throw out some ideas and provide a kind of brief overview of how to go about seeking contact. Whether you wish to pursue any of them is up to you, but if you do, be prepared for some different and sometimes unnerving experiences.

CHANNELING AND MEDIUMS

"Channeling" is a very loose term applied to a wide variety of observed results. Channeling is what a medium does. A medium is someone who can act as an intermediary between this reality and some manifestation of another, "other side" reality. This can take many forms and is something to approach with healthy skepticism, especially when we are talking about contacting the dead.

There is an enormous variety in what comes through with channeling. Ancient masters, alien civilizations, ascended and enlightened beings, teachers on other planes of existence, spirits of all kinds, and the souls of the departed are just some of the phenomena presented through mediums. It is safe to say that not all of these reported messages come from the other side.

A big problem in separating fact from well-intentioned and unconscious fiction lies within the nature of the unconscious mind, which has a psychic life and existence all its own, quite unnoticed by the waking mind. It takes intention and training to see and understand the unconscious. Most people don't pay any attention to it. The result is that when something from the unconscious mind crosses the barrier into consciousness, it is subject to misinterpretation, especially if the breakthrough seems to be communication from another plane of existence. Someone can honestly think they are in touch with someone who has crossed over, when in fact they are listening to the unconscious creation of their own psyche. It can be hard to tell the difference between genuine communication and the inner dialogue.

Some mediums with actual psychic ability may be "reading" the thoughts and feelings of their client. They translate the message as coming from the other side when it really is an unconscious, psychic response to something the client knows from personal experience. In its own way, that is just as strange as the real thing, but it is not a connection to the dead. There are genuine mediums, but they are few and far between.

Mediumship reached its popular peak during the latter part of the nineteenth century and the early part of the twentieth. Under the banner of the Spiritualism movement, many well-known and reputable people eagerly sought contact with the other side. The preferred vehicle was the séance, where groups would gather for an evening with someone who claimed the powers of contact. Strange and amazing things would happen as the room darkened. Figures, shapes, and apparitions appeared; furniture moved about; strange sounds filled the air; and soon messages for someone present would come through the medium.

Unfortunately, almost all of these phenomena were fraudulent, skillful illusions of accomplished con artists bent on relieving the gullible and wealthy of their money. The practice of holding séances fell into disrepute as the fakes were exposed. Genuine mediums lost credibility in the general rush to condemnation.

Mediums fall into two broad categories: those who remain conscious when communicating advice or messages from the other side, and those who enter a trance state. Probably the best-known example of a trance-state medium in America and the West is Edgar Cayce, mentioned earlier. Many tests, some disrespectful and painful, proved that Cayce was indeed in a deep and altered state of awareness while giving readings to the people seeking his help. In the trance state, Cayce offered cures and advice that proved successful if faithfully followed.

Trance mediumship is an ancient and honored tradition in many societies, but not in ours. Partly that is because of the many false mediums that preyed on the unsuspecting in years past. Partly it is because we are not comfortable when confronted with the full face of the mysterious reaching out to us from the other side. We prefer a more brightly lit and rational context for life.

The rise of the Age of Reason and the ascension of the scientific method diminished the trance phenomenon to an interesting anthropological footnote, confined to indigenous and "primitive" societies. Regardless of how the skeptics and scientists choose to see it, categorizing the trance state as pathological or as just an interesting cultural ritual does not change the reality of the phenomenon, nor does it diminish its power.

Every tribal society has a place for the trance state. Whether it is practiced by a Native American medicine man (or woman), a Siberian shaman, or an African elder, the trance state is honored by all tribal cultures as a means of touching the other side. A trance state can be natural or induced, brought on by innate ability, through ritual, or with the aid of psychogenic drugs. The entrance into altered states of consciousness was (and is) considered a key part of the individual's spiritual process, a milestone of personal development, and a measure of one's ability to connect with the spiritual foundations of the tribal culture.

It is not just tribal peoples who have respected the power of trance. In the classical eras of Greece and Rome, there existed a long tradition of consulting trance mediums for advice. The ancients built temples specifically for seeking and receiving

advice from the other side, focused in the person of an oracle—
a trained trance medium.

We are more likely to be comfortable (if that is the right word)
with the conscious type of medium, someone who maintains a
perfectly aware and interactive presence with us. These are the
folks we see on television and whose books we avidly devour.

You may have heard of James Van Praagh, a famous channel
to the other side. Van Praagh has written an interesting book
about his life and experiences as an open "phone line" to the
spirit world.[14] There is a consistency to the stories and experiences that Van Praagh brings through, the same kind of consistency that appears in the dreams you have encountered in these
pages. The common themes are love and comfort, pain relieved,
hurts and illness mended, renewal of life, and fulfilling existence on the other side of death.

Sometimes the messages are even more specific, offering
information no one knew except the deceased. Van Praagh's
book is full of such stories, convincing to anyone except the most
hardened and closed-minded skeptic. Life after death exists,
and that is the truth of it.

I'll share a story with you about a woman I know who is a "natural" medium. She has had a lot of difficulty accepting her ability. She is skeptical about the accuracy of what comes through
but is willing to listen. Here is the story.

Tell Him to Come Be with My Girls

*I was visiting a friend in Los Angeles—we were staying in
a hotel. My husband called me to tell me that my Aunt Jane
had died. That night, I was lying in bed getting ready to
sleep when I felt a peculiar buzzing sensation, and a kind
of pressure. It's hard to describe, but that is always the feeling I get when something is trying to come through to me. It
usually happens when I am not focused on anything and
when I am relaxed.*

Anyway, I got this message from my Aunt Jane. It felt like her. She wanted my father to come to her funeral. "Tell him to come and be with my girls," she seemed to say. The message was repeated several times.

I thought about it for a while and then called my father, who hates funerals. I knew he didn't want to go. He told me on the phone that he would think about it.

I lay down again. After a while, I again felt that feeling of pressure, and I knew it was my Aunt Jane. "Tell him to come and be with my girls," she said.

I got up again and called my father to repeat the message. Again, he said he would consider it. He told me he believed the message. But he never did go to that funeral.

You can lead a horse to water, but you can't make him drink. A message can come through loud and clear, but that does not mean anyone will act on it. We have free will, and those on the other side cannot make us do anything we do not want to do.

Here is a fascinating story from a real medium. From time to time, she can actually see people in the room who have passed on and has often acted as a bridge of communication with the other side. I know her well and know she is authentic. In this story, someone she was not acquainted with in life came to her at night, woke her up, and insisted she get a message to his family. When you read it, you will see why.

Joan's Father and the Attempted Suicide

One night about thirteen years ago, I was visited in a dream by a handsome elderly man. He introduced himself to me as the father of my friend Joan. Joan is a very successful realtor, wife and mother, church board member, and divinity student. The man was a kindly, no-nonsense person who insisted that I awaken from my dream, turn on the tape recorder, and speak into the recorder exactly what he intended to tell me.

I ungraciously replied that I could remember whatever he wanted to say and that I wasn't interested in getting up, since it was the middle of the night! Besides, what could be so important that he had to awaken a complete stranger and insist she get up immediately?

He was quite persistent and told me he was going to stay in my dream until I helped him. No one in his family could see him since he was on the other side and had recently left his body without saying good-bye to his wife and daughters. They were distraught but not speaking about it, and he hated to see them suffer. Furthermore, there was an emergency aspect to the story. I would be rendering more help than I realized by following his request.

"Oh, all right, I'll wake up and help you," I told him. Since my husband was still sleeping beside me, I took the tape recorder from the floor beside the bed. My intention was to go to another room and record the message. Joan's father then appeared beside my bed and said, "I'll tell you exactly what to say when you turn on the recorder. Then, first thing in the morning, call Joan and tell her what has happened, that I have contacted you, and please take the tape to her so she can play it for herself and her mother.

"Tell them that if they could see me as you can I'd come to them, but they don't have mediumistic abilities as you do. They may be unhappy that they have to hear my message secondhand. Please relay these three things to Joan: I love all three of them—Joan, her sister, and her mother. I will love them forever, and we will be reunited again when they finish up on the earth plane.

"My death by pneumonia was ordained. I did not abandon them by leaving them. My time was up. Joan's mother recently had an accident with the car. She ran into a tree, not by accident, but because she was trying to commit suicide. She feels she cannot live without me. She still has work to do on earth and must not try to end her life again. I can see her and am watching over her."

As I had promised, I taped the message and took it to Joan the next day. She was very upset and wondered why her beloved father would come to me, a complete stranger, instead of to a family member. I explained, but she seemed peeved. Finally, she told me that her mother had indeed crashed her car into a tree and was extremely depressed, as was she.

A few days later, I attended a gathering at Joan's house. After the other guests had left, I saw her father standing beside a lovely grandfather clock. I told her that her father was standing beside the clock, looking fondly at her.

"He's very handsome, white-haired, has glasses and a square face and looks a bit like Malcolm Forbes," I said.

"That's him! That's my father. You're right, I can't see him. He made that grandfather clock for me by hand and I'm very sentimental about it. Thank you!

"I have been wondering lately if God is real, if there actually is an afterlife, and what the whole point of living is if we have to endure so much suffering. This is very meaningful to Jim and me."

We must not abuse the gift of life by rejecting it. It is not a good thing to do, spiritually speaking, and there are tough lessons to go through if we forget and succeed in killing ourselves in a moment of depression. Joan's father was giving his wife good advice, as well as letting his family know that everything was in good order and as it should be.

Why didn't he come to his wife in a dream? Who knows, but he did find a way to communicate, choosing someone psychically sensitive to take the message where it had to go.

If you choose to consult a medium because you would like to connect to the other side, please be cautious and take the experience with several grains of salt. Anyone who wants to hear words of love from someone who has passed on also wants to believe a connection can be made. It can, but you must exercise discrimination. It is possible for a skilled professional to discover a great deal about you and your loved ones simply by asking simple questions and observing your responses.

INTO THE MIRROR

A very ancient method for connecting to the other side is called scrying. Scrying is the practice of using a polished or reflective surface, such as a bowl of water or a mirror, to open the door of perception to a different reality. It is another way to establish an altered state of consciousness. This is the method reportedly used by Nostradamus, the famous seer of the sixteenth century. Nostradamus was able to part the veil between past, present, and future with scrying. Gazing into his polished bowl of still, silvery liquid, he foresaw many events far into a future he could not truly understand. The death of kings, the rise of Nazi Germany, the Napoleonic wars, disasters and wonders of every kind—he found all of these in a simple bowl. Fearing the power of the Catholic Inquisition, he encrypted his prophecies and messages in coded and complex rhymes. Centuries have passed since he looked into his bowl, and time has proved his visions accurate more than once.

Scrying is the technique used by the reader of a crystal ball— the polished surface of the ball provides a screen for something to appear. You don't have to own a crystal ball if you want to explore scrying. It is possible to use an ordinary mirror to achieve a very powerful experience of something. The question is, what is it that is seen? Just as the unconscious may emerge clothed in the garb of messages from beyond, it may appear full blown in the mirror where it can be seen and directly experienced.

I spent over a year working twenty to thirty minutes twice a day with a mirror, as a meditation and exploration of the unconscious. It is not something everyone might want to do! I have sometimes used a brief version of the technique in conferences and workshops focused on personal discovery. When working with another person, the exercise is called "Trespasso." I am not sure why it is called that—perhaps because it "trespasses" upon ordinary reality, or perhaps there is a connotation with the ancient mystery schools of Italy and Greece.

When used with a mirror, the Trespasso method is a kind of scrying, an effort to see beyond the ordinary limitations of sight into some other reality. In other times, people tried to call up images of the dead and communicate with them. That was not my purpose when I was practicing the technique. My purpose was to explore and take whatever appeared. What usually appears is the unconscious mind, which is full of powerful visual content. That said, the Trespasso technique may be used to gain possible access to the other side.

After some consideration, I am going to give the technique here.[15] I do not recommend the practice of this exercise for most people, as it is best applied in conjunction with other forms of meditation, centering, and spiritual protection. If you decide to try it, be sure you do not overdo it. Do not do this exercise if you are taking drugs of any kind, including any of the many pre-scription drugs commonly given as antidepressants. Do not do this exercise if you have been drinking or if you have any serious health condition, or any condition whatsoever that affects your vision. You are responsible for what you choose to do and for the results you get, so bear this in mind if you decide to try it.

THE MIRROR EXERCISE

1. Place a comfortable chair at a slight angle about two or three feet before a large mirror. The mirror doesn't have to be full length, just large enough to have a good view of your upper body, head, and face.

2. Get a candle. You will be working in a darkened room with only the candle to provide light. If you are uncomfortable with a candle, use a small night-light somewhere in the

room. Dim lighting is necessary. You want to see yourself and the room behind you in the mirror, but you do not want any strong or reflected light.

3. Darken the room so that the only light available is the candle or night-light. Be sure you will not be interrupted by the telephone, pets, etc.

4. The key to this exercise involves breaking down your normal sense of vision. The way to do this is through fixing your sight on something and then "freezing" it there. This means you cannot blink, as the movement of the eyelids will restore normal visual modes.

5. Not blinking is difficult at first and will cause tears to start. You must avoid wiping the tears away or blinking, or movement of ANY KIND when doing the exercise. So, make sure you are comfortable before you start.

6. Focus on a point somewhere on your face in the mirror. I suggest the forehead, or perhaps an ear. Notice that although the light is dim, you can see all the details of your face and of the room, reflected clearly in the mirror.

7. When you are ready to begin and have picked a point of focus, hold your body completely still and do not blink. Fix your vision on the point you have chosen. Do not be alarmed when tears begin to flow.

8. Stay with it. You will probably have trouble at first keeping your eyes fixed without blinking or moving from the point of focus. If you move or blink, simply begin again. It takes strong intention to move past the discomfort of overriding the blink reflex.

9. After some time without moving or blinking, you will begin to see things in the mirror. Do not be alarmed at what you see. For example, you may see yourself become old and withered, even see the skull beneath the outer flesh. You may see a sequence of figures, young and old. You may see the form of someone who has passed to the other side. You may see yourself in some kind of past-life situation. You may

see yourself in another time and place entirely. You may see nothing.

10. After twenty minutes or so, or sooner if you wish, close your eyes and rest them. Take your time in returning from this exercise.

11. Take time to write down your impressions, feelings, thoughts, and any other details of your experience.

This is a powerful exercise, with roots in Tibet and in the Sufi traditions of the mystical path of Islam. It is a mystery school teaching for training and disciplining the outer mind, revealing some of the secrets of the unconscious mind. Because this exercise breaks down normal perception, what you perceive in the mirror is not part of normal reality. Therein lies the power of the teaching.

I advise caution with this technique, and, if possible, the guidance of a compassionate teacher. Any exercise that accesses the inner self can have far-reaching effects. It is possible to get more than you asked for.

RAYMOND MOODY, M.D.

Raymond Moody is a very popular author who has created an environment for scrying that seems to help people reconnect with the dead. He has written several books, among them *Life After Life* and *Reunions*. Dr. Moody has a facility in Alabama where people can come and explore this ancient technique. I have not experienced his work, but it seems to me to be a variation on the exercise given above, although not as strenuous, using a mirror to connect to the other side.

Dr. Moody has built a small room with a mirror, dimly lit, where one can sit and see in the mirror (or not) the form and appearance of those who have gone on. Is it a true appearance? Is it the projection of the unconscious mind? I don't know, but many people (including Dr. Moody) are convinced that the dead return and are seen in the mirror.

There is a very famous spiritual question, one asked of students and seekers for centuries. I do not recall where I first heard it, but it seems appropriate to mention it here.

In the high mountains of the Himalayas, prayer flags mark the passes and many other sites. Prayer flags are long strips of cloth inscribed with prayers. It is windy in the mountains, especially at the passes, which are sometimes dangerous and difficult to cross. The wind keeps the flags moving constantly, sending the prayers to whatever beings may be listening or paying attention. The old question for the seeker goes like this:

When you see the flag blowing in the wind, what is it that moves?
Is it the flag, or is it the wind?

I could stretch this out and place the answer at the end of the book, but I won't do that to you. Think about it for a moment. What moves, the flag or the wind? There are several answers, but only one is correct from a spiritual teaching point of view. The answer is this:

Neither. What moves is your mind.

In the mirror, what moves may be your mind or it may be a genuine visitation. Either way, the experience is real enough.

ASKING FOR A DREAM

Most people will not want to try the mirror exercise given above for many reasons. It is one of the more uncomfortable ways to go about seeking contact with the other side, and it can be troubling to know exactly what it is that is seen in the mirror. There is, however, one very accessible and easily practiced technique for making contact—dreams. After all, this entire book is about dreams of one kind or another. We can hope for a dream of return, and we can seek it out.

It is not hard to seek a dream. It does require some thought and intention, just like anything else we consider important in our life. Of course, we have to teach ourselves to notice and remember our dreams. If we cannot remember them, they will not do us much good.

Many metaphysical schools talk about the experiences of the dream body. Think of the dream body as a separate, aware extension of self, without the constraints of physical form. That means the dream body can travel with ease to places the physical body could never go, adventuring far from home. The journey takes place in the astral realm. In the astral, we are told, it is possible to make contact with those who have gone on before us.

I know people who say that they travel regularly in the astral, while dreaming. These folks describe varied and interesting experiences ranging from the most mundane to the most spiritual. I also know accomplished psychics who talk about the astral realm. It is real, but what is it? Like the images appearing in the mirror, it can be hard to make sense of what is seen.

I prefer to keep it simple, and perhaps you do, too. Simple means that we don't worry about the truth or untruth of dream bodies, the astral realm, or any of the complex metaphysics that generally accompany discussion of these alternative realities. Simple means we ask for a dream, take what we get, and prepare ourselves to record and understand whatever comes forward.

It is not always easy to understand a dream, and this book is not meant to teach interpretation. True dreams of return don't seem to require much interpretation, which is one way of evaluating any dream that does come through. If it features the form of a departed loved one but is full of complicated symbolism and confusing actions, perhaps it is "just" a psychological dream. Even so, these can be wonderfully healing and inspiring. In my experience, most true dreams of return are very straightforward, with clear and direct messages of love and comfort.

How do you get a dream? If you are a person who has no trouble remembering dreams, then this may not seem like a new idea. Many people, though, do not remember dreams well or even at all. Dreams are stored in very short-term memory, and the images dissipate rapidly on waking. Everyone does dream; if dreaming is prevented, serious consequences result. Many sleep-lab studies focused on the rapid eye movement (REM) state, where most dreaming occurs, as well as anecdotal and real-life experiences, confirm this fact. Dreaming is necessary for mental and physical health.

SEEDING A DREAM OF RETURN

It helps to be somewhat proficient in remembering dreams and have some practice in paying attention to them if you want to incubate a dream of return. The unconscious responds to external events and stimuli, so the first step is to get the idea across to yourself that you want to remember and record a dream. Here's how to go about seeding a dream of return.

• Prepare as if you are confident about remembering the dream. That means making sure you are ready and willing to wake and record the dream when it comes. Keep a pad of paper and pen or a recorder by your bed, just for capturing dreams.

• Think it through—what are you trying to accomplish? If you are seeking reconnection to someone on the other side, why are you doing so? What is your motivation? What, if anything, would you say to your loved ones if they suddenly appeared? You already have an idea, or it would not even occur to you to want contact, but it is necessary to clarify your thoughts and intention. This helps both you and the one you want to contact.

- Notice if you have any ideas or thoughts that might get in the way of letting that person appear. Are you fearful of the idea that the dead return? Are you upset because there is something you need from the other, like a message of love or forgiveness? Are you angry with the other for leaving (or any other reason)? Is there unfinished business between you that requires resolution? These are perfectly natural thoughts and feelings, and they can create an obstacle to communication. As best you can, please set these considerations aside. This will also help you focus on asking for a dream.

- Give yourself a self-hypnotic suggestion when you go to bed about the dream you are seeking. Self-hypnosis is an easy and natural state for all of us. We spend a lot of time, more than you might think, in light, self-induced hypnotic states. Giving yourself a suggestion is easy. Place your hands on your chest, right over your breastbone, and say your suggestion out loud to yourself. For example, you could tell yourself, "Tonight I will dream of ———," placing the name of the beloved in the blank space. As you do this, press a finger into your chest at the same time. Continue to repeat this aloud to yourself until you have run through all ten fingers. Then go to sleep. Repeat this every night until you get a dream.

- Be very patient with yourself. It can take days or weeks for a dream to appear, but if you persevere, you will meet with success sooner or later.

Seeking information or connection in dreams is another technique of spiritual discovery that has been around for a long time. It has been practiced since mankind began dreaming and thinking about the meaning of life and death. You can use it, too, with success.

LUCID DREAMING

Lucid dreaming (also known as conscious dreaming) is another legacy of early shamanic and spiritual practices and is part of the nature of our fundamental humanity. Humans and animals both dream, but only humans try to make sense of dreams. Only humans can apply consciousness to a dream as they are dreaming. Only humans can become aware in a dream and use that knowledge for some specific purpose.

Lucid dreaming was once an esoteric and obscure practice, but it has come into popular awareness during the last few decades as a psychological tool and as a means of exploring self-awareness. It is a way to explore any subject. Once you know you are dreaming, you can create almost any experience. Like in all dreams, the experience feels real. Feats of athletic prowess, flying, great sex—all of these and more become possible. It is also possible to meet with the dead.

There are several proven techniques for initiating conscious dreaming. This is the next step beyond regular dreaming. Just as when seeking a regular dream, you need to ask yourself a few questions. Before doing anything, it is a good idea to think through what you want to accomplish and why you are trying to wake up within your dreams. So that is the first step: Get clear about what it is you want to do with this powerful tool of awareness. What is your purpose in starting this practice? I suggest that at first you content yourself with becoming aware that you are dreaming while you are within your dream. That is a major success and the prerequisite for further exploration.

Once you achieve the ability to become aware in dreams, it is time to train yourself to accomplish your desired goals. If all you want is a fantasy trip, then it will be relatively easy. Think about what you want and the dream will provide some context and experience that fits your desire. Many people go no further with lucid dreaming than visiting the inner pleasure dome their minds can provide. There are other possibilities, however.

Lucid dreaming appears in many different cultures as part of the road to spiritual discovery. In Buddhist teachings there is "dream yoga." It is the practice of consciousness when asleep and dreaming. Since Buddhist philosophy teaches the impermanence and illusory nature of all things, learning how to be aware in dreams provides one more way for the student to experience the teachings. Because dreams are just another kind of illusion, according to Buddhist thought, mastering dreams gives practice in mastering the outer illusion we consider to be reality. Lucid dreaming is an exercise in spiritual awareness and awakening.

Shamanic traditions use conscious dreaming as a means of discovery and accumulating personal power. For example, dreams are used as part of healing rituals. The shaman might go looking for a medicinal herb or cure for sickness within a dream, or might seek the aid of a power animal or advice from the spirit world. That includes the dead. To the expanded and mystical mind that emerges in altered states (and conscious dreaming is an altered state), there is no separation between the dead and the living, the spirit world and our own. They are just different dimensions of one reality. It is all about perception and about learning how to alter perception so that a different reality appears. That is what happens in the mirror exercise. The key to connection to the other side lies in altered perception.

The leading edge of scientific knowledge deals with different realities of perception. For example, quantum physics reveals that everything is appearing out of nothing, a kind of spontaneous, random, and ongoing creation of all existence as we know it. This is the borderline between realities, where physics meets God. Light itself is a perceptual and physical contradiction, existing as both discreet particles and continuous waves, depending on how one looks at it. How can it be both? The answer, once we get past the efforts to define and rationalize, is that it is both because it is. So, too, the reality of altered perception found in conscious dreaming states. Beyond the fantasies of the untamed ego lies a gateway into other dimensions, a doorway to the other side.

HOW TO BEGIN EXPLORING CONSCIOUS DREAMING

If you have Internet and computer access, you can find a lot of information about conscious dreaming on the Web. Start with the Lucidity Institute (www.lucidity.com), founded by Stephen LaBerge, Ph.D. A search using the words "lucid dreaming" will quickly reveal many different sites to explore. These sites will introduce you to lucid dreaming and point you in the direction of further information if you want to get it. You can also buy light devices on the Web to help initiate lucidity. These devices can help you achieve consciousness in dreams.

Light devices look like sleeping masks, which is exactly what they are, except that they also contain low light–emitting diodes triggered by REM sleep. As we enter the dream state, our eyes begin to move rapidly back and forth, tracking the images of the dream. With the light device, the movement activates the diodes, causing a low, repeated flashing that registers as you sleep and dream. When you see the flashing light in the dream, it is a signal to awaken (within the dream) and begin the conscious exploration. This is the technique favored in sleep labs studying conscious dreaming.

A second tried-and-true technique for initiating lucid dreams requires no external aids. Learn to find a visual cue in your dreams. While awake, decide on something that will remind you that, when you see it in a dream, you are dreaming. The classic example is to use a body cue such as finding your hands or looking at your feet. This is the technique taught to Carlos Castaneda by the Yaqui shaman Don Juan. Castaneda's famous series of books, written over a period of twenty years, details his studies in altered awareness with the mysterious teacher Don

Juan in Mexico. At least a portion of these books is true, and one of the true parts is Don Juan's teaching about dreaming. Don Juan told Castaneda to find his hands in his dream and, once he did, to look around and observe what he saw.[16] That was good advice for Castaneda, and it is good advice for you.

Choose your hands, your feet, or something else as a visual cue. It can be anything that speaks to you. If you are familiar with the television series *Star Trek: Voyager,* you may remember an episode that illustrates the point. Commander Chakotay, the first officer of the starship, has taught himself to realize he is dreaming if he sees the full moon. That is a good cue, because *Voyager* is lost in a distant quadrant of the galaxy, several thousand light years away from anything that looks like Earth's full moon. Therefore, if he were seeing the full moon as from Earth, he would surely be dreaming.

In the TV episode, a hostile alien species tricks the crew of *Voyager* into falling asleep. The crew members do not know they are asleep, because they are dreaming that they are awake. Of course, they will eventually die if they do not wake up. Caught in the illusion, Chakotay suddenly looks outside the portal window and sees the full moon floating in outer space—and, realizing that he is asleep and dreaming, wakes up. Ultimately this leads to his saving the day and outwitting the hostile aliens.

You can choose any cue. Then you must set your intention to wake up in your dreams. You can do this is a few ways. Here is a simple sequence to follow if you would like to try this technique.

Initiating Conscious Dreaming

• Choose a visual cue that will serve to remind you that you are dreaming if you see it in a dream. Hands are a good choice, but it can be anything you like. The moon, a special stone—anything that speaks to you. Your hands or feet are good because you do not usually focus on these in dreams. Don't choose something that might be a common dream symbol, like someone you know or your dog.

• Prepare yourself to remember any dreams you might have. You don't have to study dreams if you don't want to, but you won't have much luck with lucid dreaming if you are unable to remember your dreams in the first place. Be prepared to record your dreams in some way, with a notebook or recorder by your bed. That sends a cue to the unconscious that you are serious. If you want to learn how to work with dreams, read one of my other books, *What Your Dreams Can Teach You* (New York: M. Evans, 2001).

• As with initiating regular dreams, give yourself a self-hypnotic suggestion before going to sleep. An autosuggestion is something you tell yourself with the intention of producing a specific result. For example, you could tell yourself, "I will find my hands in my dream and be aware that I am dreaming." Say this out loud to yourself ten times. Each time you say it, press one of your fingers into your chest. This helps anchor the suggestion. Then go to sleep.

• Be patient! You are trying to teach yourself an advanced technique of consciousness. It may be very easy for you, or it may take some time. It took Castaneda a long time before he finally found his hands in a dream, but when he did, he rapidly learned to enter his dreams with conscious awareness. If you are diligent and genuinely interested, you will succeed.

• When you succeed, try to remain conscious of your surroundings, without altering the dream. This gets tricky, because the ego loves the idea of altering dreams. After all, if you could create anything you wanted, wouldn't you be tempted to do so? Becoming aware in dreams is a little bit like becoming God. It is also a trap if you are interested in more than illusion.

- With practice, you can remain in a state of lucidity for longer and longer periods. Develop tricks, like spinning on one foot or drinking a glass of water (in the dream) to remain conscious when you feel your awareness slipping back into an ordinary dream state.

- Once you have learned to do these things, you can use the lucid state to attempt making contact with the other side. Be easy with yourself and try not to be disappointed if you don't succeed quickly.

Lucid dreaming can be wonderfully pleasant and engaging and can occur spontaneously. Here is a typical comment from a lucid dreamer.

It Just Happened...

I do experience many pleasant dreams and I remember them quite clearly, as I am a lucid and vivid dreamer. I am (most times) aware that I am dreaming and can go into my dreams and change them. For instance, if I know that I am having a nightmare, the nightmare will continue until the end, and I will tell myself that it was only a nightmare. . . . start from the beginning and change whatever it is that I don't feel comfortable with. At times however, I cannot change them and am not aware that I am dreaming. The ability to "know" that I am dreaming seemed to come naturally . . . it just happened

The key to success with any of these techniques is focus, intention, and preparation. *Focus*, because you must be very single-minded about what you want to achieve. *Intention*, because that is the energizing force that gives focus impact and reality. *Preparation*, because you must prepare yourself psychically and mentally for the technique you are going to employ, as well as take care of physical requirements like mirrors, lighting, light devices, or recording materials. I want to emphasize that the ideas presented in this chapter *will* work, if you learn how to apply them. Since we are talking about these ideas in the context of parting the veil to the other side, you need to have a clear and purposeful intention if you decide to try them out. Remember, we are talking about alternate dimensions of reality not generally open to us. When we succeed in crossing the boundary, it is a good idea to be prepared for surprises.

Chapter 8

The End Is the Beginning

I applied my heart to what I observed
And learned a lesson from what I saw.
—PROVERBS 24:32

W E HAVE MANY LESSONS TO LEARN about life, death, and life after death. Something is going on here that we do not understand. Science cannot give us concrete and specific answers or information about what happens after we die. Postdeath existence is not in the scientific area of expertise. However, we can find the answers in dreams and visions, messages and truths from the other side.

The best science can do is give us a measurement of something that changes at death, although even this is controversial. I have heard about a measurement of the soul. That measurement is 21 grams. Twenty-one grams of weight (not very much) seems to be lost at the instant of death. Does the soul weigh 21 grams? Something leaves at death, something changes, and that something seems to weigh 21 grams. Whatever it is, it is there until death and then it is gone.

I don't know if the soul weighs 21 grams. I suspect the soul doesn't weigh anything, since it must be composed of pure spiritual energy, but perhaps I am wrong. I do know one thing, though, and that is the psychic fact of thousands of years of similar stories and dreams of the dead returning. There is a huge body of consistent, anecdotal evidence of life after death and of the return in dreams and visions of those who have passed on.

What stories come from across the divide? When people return in dreams from the other side, they bring the same message. Life goes on and love awaits us on the other side of death's door.

Once we leave our physical form, we experience a very different kind of existence. Illness and the cares of the body fall away. We attain a state of health and well-being, radiant and strong, even if we never had that experience when alive. We realize things we only suspected or never considered during our brief stay on the physical plane. We learn things after we die. We discover we are loved and that we are not alone. There are beings with us all the time, guides and teachers who protect us and push us gently toward greater spiritual awareness.

Existence here on Earth appears to be a school of consciousness, the oldest and largest mystery school of them all. The lessons are always the same. Love, forgiveness, service, and compassion for life and our human brothers and sisters comprise the core curriculum. We find it hard to put these lessons into practice, and I suppose that is why we have to go through the experience more than once. Reincarnation helps us get it right.

The evolution of our individual souls and the expression of soul values through physical incarnation are the greatest mysteries of the universe. These mysteries will be resolved when we die. It is foolish to argue about them among ourselves. Those arguments usually end up creating rigid barriers of theological disagreement that prevent understanding and ultimately lead to war and destruction.

I find it comforting to realize that regardless of the disagreements here on Earth, the afterlife reality seems quite unaffected by all the noise and drama of the human ego. We die, we change realities, we move on.

Sometimes people have to endure a challenging experience after death. Someone who took his own life might have to spend time in an unhappy place. Knowing we have made a serious mistake and having to wait out the time needed to correct it can be torment enough. Stories told to dreamers by people who are having a difficult time in the afterlife focus on their understanding that they are correcting a mistake and that when that is accomplished, things will be better. Could these kinds of dreams and visions be the experiential basis for the idea of hell and punishment after death?

Returnees do not speak of punishment, because that is never a theme on the other side. They speak of lessons and of regret for some of their actions. It is only here in our physical world that we imagine punishment awaits for the mistakes we must inevitably make during our lives. Punishment and love are not consistent with each other, in spite of theology to the contrary. A loving God does not throw most of the world into eternal torment for any reason, including practicing different forms of worship and prayer. It is the worship and prayer that count, not the words or form.

This world we live in is only one facet, one expression, of an infinite form with many dimensions. Immanuel Kant, the German philosopher of the eighteenth century, thought of the other side as a kind of change of perspective that takes place when we die. Like the ancient Egyptians, Kant thought that life went on very much as before, just in a different kind of spiritual substance.[17]

Many of the dreams in these pages bear this out. People return to their loved ones after death. What do they say? Things are good here, I feel great, don't worry, I'll be looking out for you, I will always love you, I won't see you for a while (that one is interesting, isn't it?), and more. They say they are learning things, and sometimes that is very apparent to the dreamer. When you know someone well, you notice things about that person that change over time, especially if it has been a while since you last saw him or her.

I've Changed and Grown

Jim was my neighbor growing up. We were friends and went to high school dances together. He committed suicide when we were about twenty-one. I have had several dreams of him over the years where he came to me. He seemed fine, but always sort of the same energy. Still shy and quiet.

Recently I had a dream where Jim showed up. He looked good, looked the same in body as I remember him, young and healthy. But he was different, and he told me so. He said he was doing very well and that he had changed and grown. He had matured emotionally and spiritually and was much happier. I could feel it was true and he did seem to have grown. His energy was different. That was the end of the dream.

I told the dream to his sister, who was touched by it and grateful. She, in turn, told her mother, who was also very open and grateful for the information. I find it interesting that he stays in touch with me this way and figure it must be that he wants me to share it with his family.

Some of the most profound experiences come to people just as they lie dying. We have a lot to learn from these dreams and visions. Deathbed visions are particularly moving, but it is easy for the living to dismiss them as hallucinations of a failing brain or side effects of medications. One of my favorite movies of all time features a scene where the dying father, a bitter and hard man, suddenly sees the beauty of the light as he comes to the moment of his death. *Resurrection* (1975) is a movie everyone should see, because it carries the real energy of unconditional and compassionate love. It stars Ellen Burstyn as a healer brought into her abilities by a near-death experience. It is only a movie (although it is loosely based on the experiences of a genuine healer), but it is a wonderful portrayal of a psychic reality. It gives a feeling for how thin the barrier is between that reality and this one. It is a story of love and forgiveness.

What is it that we all seek and desire? I think it is as simple as one word—love. Love is the message we hear from the other side. Our loved ones return to let us know all is well. They don't need to do that for their own benefit—they already know all is well. They do it for ours, to help us handle our grief, to reassure us, to let us know we are loved. What makes life worthwhile is love. We just need to find it or touch it.

Dreams of return are signs of the eternal mystery of love, the mystery of the divine. Everyone is loved, everyone. When the door to the other side opens in dreams, that is what we discover.

Sometimes we get a message in dreams that comes straight from the other side without confronting us with images of loved ones gone. I'd like to close this book with one of those dreams.

Two Sets of Lenses

I am looking at two sets of lenses. One set is labeled "Fear," the other, "Love."

I pick up the lenses marked "Fear," and hold them up to my eyes. When I look through them, everything looks weird and creepy. People look strange and distorted, angry. The colors and the background look dark and strange. It is very creepy.

Then I pick up the lenses labeled "Love." I hold them up to my eyes and suddenly everything bursts into bloom! I am looking at beautiful fields of flowers, stretching as far as I can see.

Dreams from the Other Side

In the middle of the fields I see a message, written large and clear in red roses, set among all the other flowers. The message reads, "LOVE LIFE. FEAR NOT DEATH."

Love life, fear not death. Perhaps we should write these words down where we will see them, to remind ourselves of the truth they convey. There is nothing to fear. There is only love, and we can choose to see life through the lenses of love. Then we discover that death is but an instant of transition, our gateway into another dimension of existence, existing side by side with our own. It is just the other side of life, a place of learning, spirit, and healing.

May spirit bless you and fill your life with love and understanding.

APPENDIX

.◆..◆..◆.

DEALING WITH GRIEF

I WOULD LIKE TO SHARE a few thoughts with you about grief, just in case you are reading this book because you are, or someone you know is, grieving. After all, "the other side" is a phrase we associate with death and separation, a way to talk about the mystery of life and the meaning of death. There are many reasons to read a book about the other side, and personal loss is one of them.

Whether the grief is ours or someone else's, there are some things we can do and some things we can understand about grieving that can help us through it. Something important to remember about grief is this: It creates a fundamental upheaval in the life of the person who is affected. The kind of personal loss that produces grief is life changing in some way. We are not talking about just being sad or upset about something. We grieve when faced with devastating and irrevocable loss. At the top of the list is the loss of a loved one.

Some cultures have an honored and ancient tradition of public and emotional grieving, grieving that helps family and community accept the loss of a loved one. In the West, our culture is

193

uncomfortable with expressions of grief. Mourning is not something we do well. We are not prepared by custom for the reality of grief, nor do we have much of a tradition supporting public, emotional expression of our feelings.

The first thing to know about grief is that there is no standard timetable for healing; the second is that we have to honor and acknowledge our feelings. Mourning the dead means admitting loss in a way that removes any illusions that it isn't so. It can take many years to allow mourning to begin.

It is normal and natural to slip into denial about death. Confronted with the finality of loss, something in us needs time to comprehend and accept what has happened. If you or someone you know is grieving, there are some simple things to do and remember. These things provide a framework, a temporary structure for getting through it. It helps a little to realize that your feelings and actions are normal. It is important to remember that confusion about those feelings is a normal response.

Common Responses to Grief

Grief is so overwhelming that it can take precedence over everything else. That means we act and respond in ways not like our normal self. We do not think or feel the same way that we do when things are all right in our lives. This can show up in different ways. Below is a list of typical, normal responses.

- We lose the ability to concentrate and follow through on even simple tasks.

- We feel exhausted, used up mentally and physically. We have trouble sleeping.

- We start to talk with someone, only to forget what it was that we were going to say.

- We are overwhelmed with tears and emotion when we least expect it.

- We cry a lot.

- We feel out of control, lost on an emotional roller coaster.

- Nothing appeals to us—we lose interest in the things that previously gave us joy.

- We feel isolated and alone, even when others support and surround us.

- We find ourselves feeling angry at the one who has gone, and then feel guilty for feeling angry.

- We need to tell others stories about the one who has gone.

- We need to tell others how we felt when we heard the news or realized our loved one was gone.

- We have thoughts of suicide and joining the person who has died.

- We start to busy ourselves in routines, but find ourselves unable to complete them or we let them go entirely.

These are some of the ways we respond to the death of a loved one, some of the ways we express our grief.

Sometimes people say all the wrong things, with the best of intentions, to someone who is in the depths of grieving. The words are meant to comfort but have the opposite effect. They seem to diminish the very real feelings of grief and dismiss the one who has died, in the eyes of the person doing the grieving. They are phrases like, "God never gives us more than we can handle," or "I'm sure he's happier now," or (my favorite) "Time heals all wounds." It may be true that the passage of time helps alleviate the pain, but it takes more than time to complete grieving. Even if it were completely true, the phrase demeans the present suffering and feelings of the one left behind.

Don't be like that if you are trying to comfort the bereaved. The best thing is to recognize the depth of emotion the other is feeling and validate it for what it is, without trying to change it. There are other things we can do to support and nurture someone dealing with loss.

Do's and Don'ts for Comforting Someone Who Is Grieving

- Don't judge the way someone responds to loss. For example, some people will try to act as if everything is okay. They are quick to resume all the normal routines of life, like showing up for work or going to the movies. Sometimes doing normal things provides a sense of safety and comfort, even when there is great emotional turmoil inside.

- Do remain available to the person, for conversation or just quiet listening. People need to share their loss. If it makes you uncomfortable, perhaps you are unconsciously reacting to the potential for your own loss, your own potential meeting with grief. You are not supposed to be a counselor, just someone who is willing to listen and validate.

- Do remember that a person who is grieving can suddenly burst into tears for no apparent reason. Don't judge them, or think they should have better control of their emotions. Many simple things can remind the bereaved of their loss, triggering an emotional outburst.

- Do remember that grieving people do not function the same way they usually do. Don't expect them to act "normally."

Dealing with Grief

- Do acknowledge the loss. Although it may not be a good idea to offer platitudes and clichés like, "Time heals all wounds," you can acknowledge loss and let the grieving person know you are there and understand. That can be as simple as saying, "I'm sorry for your loss and I want you to know I care and think about you." You will find your own words—the important thing is that you let them know you care. Don't say it if you don't mean it!

- If it is appropriate, do help with things. That could be anything from showing up with lunch to helping make funeral arrangements. Ask if there is anything you can do and be prepared to follow up on your offer if there is. Don't be intrusive; just find out if there is a service you can provide.

- Don't push spirit and religion on the grief-stricken. Sometimes even very religious or spiritual people get very angry with God for awhile when a loved one dies. They are not ready to renew the connection. Let things take their natural course. Meanwhile, you can offer your own, private prayers for the other.

- Don't take things personally if the person you are trying to comfort responds with anger or indifference. It is a natural part of his or her grief.

- Do be honest with yourself about your own feelings and do your best not to let them get in the way. By that, I mean pay attention to how you feel, and notice if it is interfering with your ability to support the grieving person. For example, if you are uncomfortable with the thought of death, you might try to get the other to stop grieving so that *you* can feel better. Do you see how it works? We all do this; just notice it and set it aside.

Many people report feeling that their lost loved one is nearby or present in the room. One of the things you can do is acknowledge the other's feelings of a closeness to or presence of the dead person. They may tell you of a dream where the loved one returns. If someone gifts you with the intimacy of a dream of return, I encourage you to honor it. That dream may be exactly what will turn the tide of emotions from grief to hope.

Notes

1. I came across this story in a very interesting book by Robert L. Van de Castle, Ph.D. The book is called *Our Dreaming Mind* (New York: Ballantine Books, 1994). A great book for anyone interested in dreams.
2. *Webster's Dictionary* (New York: Pyramid Communications, 1972).
3. Marie-Louise Von Franz, *On Dreams and Death* (Boston: Shambala, 1986).
4. F. Coolidge and C. Fish, "Dreams of the Dying," *Omega Journal of Death and Dying* 14 (1): 1983-84.
5. *Ibid.*
6. Carl Sandburg, *Abraham Lincoln, The War Years*, (New York: Charles Scribner's Sons, 1949) 6: 244–245.
7. *Ibid.*
8. Carl G. Jung, *Memories, Dreams, Reflections*, ed. Aniela Jaffe (New York: Random House, 1961).
9. *Ibid.*
10. *Ibid.*
11. *Ibid.*
12. Reading 243-5, given 3 September, 1927.

13. J. Stearn, *The Search for a Soul—Taylor Caldwell's Psychic Lives* (New York: Doubleday & Company, Inc., 1973).
14. James Van Praagh, *Talking to Heaven* (New York: Penguin Putnam, 1997).
15. I first learned this technique from Brugh Joy, M.D. You may read more about it in his excellent book, *Joy's Way* (Los Angeles: J. P. Tarcher, 1978).
16. Carlos Castaneda's books about his studies and adventures form a very interesting and complete set of teachings about the shamanic world. For a look at the teachings about dreams, read *The Art of Dreaming* (New York: HarperCollins, 1993).
17. *Lectures on Metaphysics*, 1821. The reference was found in Aniela Jaffe's book, *An Archetypal Approach to Death Dreams and Ghosts* (Solothurn, Switzerland: Daimon Verlag, 1999).

Bibliography

Castaneda, Carlos. *The Art of Dreaming*. New York: HarperCollins, 1993.

Coolidge, Frederick L., and Cynthia E. Fish. "Dreams of the Dying," *Omega Journal of Death and Dying*, 14 (1): 1983–1984.

George, Leonard, Ph.D. *Alternative Realities*. New York: Facts on File, 1995.

Jaffe, Aniela, <u>An Archetypal Approach to Death Dreams and Ghosts</u>, Daimon Verlag, 1999, Solothurn.

Joy, William Brugh, M.D. *Joy's Way*. Los Angeles: J. P. Tarcher, 1978.

Jung, Carl Gustav. *Memories, Dreams, Reflections*. Edited by Aniela Jaffe. New York: Random House, 1961.

Kubler-Ross, Elizabeth. *On Life After Death*. Berkeley, California: Celestial Arts, 1991.

Miller, Robert J., ed. *The Complete Gospels*. Sonoma, California: Polebridge Press, 1992.

Miller, Sukie, Ph.D. *After Death*. New York: Touchstone, 1998.

Moody, Raymond A. Jr., M.D. *Life After Life*. New York: HarperCollins, 2001.

201

Moss, Robert. *Conscious Dreaming*. New York: Three Rivers Press, 1996.

———. *Dreamgates*. New York: Three Rivers Press, 1998.

Sandburg, Carl. *Abraham Lincoln, The War Years*. Vol. 6. New York: Charles Scribner's Sons, 1949.

Sonsino, Rifat, and Daniel B. Syme. *What Happens After I Die?* New York: UAHC Press, 1990.

Stearn, Jess. *The Search for a Soul—Taylor Caldwell's Psychic Lives*. New York: Doubleday & Company, 1973.

Sugrue, Thomas. *The Story of Edgar Cayce*. Virginia Beach: A.R.E. Press, 1997.

Van de Castle, Robert L., Ph.D. *Our Dreaming Mind*. New York: Ballantine Books, 1994.

Van Praagh, James. *Talking to Heaven*. New York: Penguin Putnam, 1997.

Von Franz, Marie-Louise. *On Dreams and Death*. Boston: Shambala, 1986.

Webster's Dictionary. New York: Pyramid Communications, 1972.

Weiss, Brian, M.D. *Through Time Into Healing*. New York: Fireside, 1993.

Index